America's Child-Care Crisis

Rethinking an Essential Business

Sarah Taylor Vanover, EdD

Gryphon House

Copyright

BULK PURCHASE

Gryphon House books are available for special premiums and sales promotions as well as for fund-raising use. Special editions or book excerpts also can be created to specifications. For details, call 800.638.0928.

DISCLAIMER

Gryphon House, Inc., cannot be held responsible for damage, mishap, or injury incurred during the use of or because of activities in this book. Appropriate and reasonable caution and adult supervision of children involved in activities and corresponding to the age and capability of each child involved are recommended at all times. Do not leave children unattended at any time. Observe safety and caution at all times.

This book is not intended to give legal or financial advice. All financial and legal opinions contained herein are from the personal research and experience of the author and are intended as educational material. Seek the advice of a qualified legal advisor or financial advisor before making legal or financial decisions.

This book is dedicated to Andrea and all my colleagues at the Kentucky Division of Child Care. Thank you for all your hard work to take care of our Kentucky children and support our child-care providers. You are appreciated!

Table of Contents

Introduction

Child care is the industry that supports all other industries. At the same time, child care is an industry whose employees are significantly underpaid and do not receive the respect they deserve for supporting young children and families. This dichotomy is the reason that our child-care programs are frequently in danger of collapse.

One of the essential tasks of child-care programs is to provide care and education for young children. Because it has been established that the largest portion of brain development occurs before a child reaches five years of age (Center on the Developing Child, 2020), we know that children must be in a learning-rich environment starting at birth to reach their full developmental potential. Quality child-care programs promote the development of the whole child, including cognitive development, language skills, motor skills, social and emotional development, and self-help skills. A child who has benefited from a high-quality early childhood education program will be much more likely to enter kindergarten prepared and to be successful in elementary school than a child who has not had the benefit of a learning-rich environment.

A second crucial job of the child-care program is allowing family members to go to work consistently without constant worry about their children's safety. When parents find a child-care program they trust, they are more likely to attend work regularly and support their family to the best of their ability. When families do not have consistent and quality child care, they are more likely to miss work or lose a job, which could have devastating effects on their economic situation.

Specialists in the field of human services may state that the health and safety of the family is much more important than whether or not a parent loses a job due to lack of child care; however, the health and safety and the economic stability of the family are linked. When a family has a consistent income, the family members are more likely to have regular health care, proper nutrition, and safe housing (Blair and Raver, 2016). A consistent income significantly reduces the level of stress in the home. All family members are more likely to have healthy social and emotional development if the family experiences lower levels of stress, which potentially reduces the chances of abuse, domestic violence, and addiction (Blair and Raver, 2016).

It is difficult to link child care directly to a positive home life for young children; however, quality child care is definitely a contributing factor to positive family life. Despite the essential need for child care in our culture, the child-care industry is by far one of the most unstable businesses in the United States. The current business structure is not working, and without changes, the situation could lead to a catastrophic breakdown affecting millions of working families.

A FRAGILE ECOSYSTEM

The Prichard Committee for Academic Excellence, an education-advocacy organization based in Lexington, Kentucky, created a webinar series during the COVID-19 pandemic called "A Fragile Ecosystem: The Impact of COVID-19 on Kentucky's Child-Care Providers." This title is a perfect description of the balancing act that child care has been performing since its creation. Even before the pandemic began, the child-care industry maintained an extremely fragile ecosystem. It has been nearly impossible to balance the needs of the child-care business with the available resources of the families it serves.

The parent perspective is that tuition is too high to maintain. When a family has its first child, instantly the parents must adjust their expenses and income to provide an additional $800 to $1,200 per month to pay for the care of their infant. In most cases, this is the largest expense that the family pays each month, exceeding the cost of their rent or mortgage. Once a family has two children in child care at one time, they often must reevaluate whether it is in their best interest for one adult to stay home to care for the children. Single-parent families must determine if there is a way to pay fixed expenses, such as food, housing, and utilities, while also paying for child care. Based on the burden that quality child care places on the family, the cost seems astronomical.

The Bureau of Labor Statistics (2018) shows that in almost two-thirds of married families both parents have jobs. America has more than 13.5 million single parents who must have an income to support their families (Bureau of Labor Statistics, 2018). Aside from simply needing to pay bills, there are other reasons for families to stay in the workforce when their children are young. Many adults are passionate about their careers and enjoy going to work. Other parents are scared that leaving the workforce, even for a couple of years, could cause them to be significantly demoted when they return to the workplace. There are also parents who utilize quality child care to prepare their children for elementary school and to take stress off of the home environment. Some families strongly believe they are better parents when they have the opportunity to have time away from their children each day. All of these reasons show why American families need access to child care.

The parent may feel that she is being financially manipulated by the child-care program; however, it is important for the family to understand all the expenses that the weekly fees cover. When a babysitter comes to a family's home, the entire fee goes directly to the individual caring for the child. The babysitter is not responsible for establishing routines, creating an attached relationship, assessing the child's development, or creating an environment filled with language opportunities. The babysitter is there to care for the child's basic needs, and she will use the family's resources (home, toys, food, and so on) to do so during the hours for which she is being paid.

A child-care program is significantly different. The number of teachers that a child interacts with during the day is based on the number of the children in the room and the required adult-to-child ratio. A child's tuition pays a small amount toward the cost of two to four teachers caring for her during the course of the day. Child-care programs pay additional expenses as well, such as rent, utilities, and insurance premiums. Also, many different consumable materials are used throughout the day, including cleaning supplies, art supplies, meals, and snacks. The administrative staff must be paid to supervise the teachers, process the finances, and make sure the facility is maintained. The toys and the playground must be kept clean and in good condition. There are always maintenance needs to consider, such as plumbing and electrical issues. Finally, the highest quality programs train their teachers on research-based practices and how to use a high-quality curriculum. All these expenses are factored into the child's weekly tuition, with the intended goal of the center's breaking even or building a reserve fund for unexpected expenses or emergencies. Truly, $200 to $250 per week is a reasonable cost to cover all these demands.

The teacher perspective is slightly different. Teachers have a high-demand job. They are not sitting at a desk resting all day. From the time they enter the classroom, their job requires their full attention; otherwise, a child could get hurt. Not only do teachers need to be diligent about meeting the basic needs of the children— changing diapers, serving meals and snacks, cleaning the classroom—but they must also plan activities that challenge the physical and cognitive development of each child in the classroom. To provide the best learning experiences, the teachers need to assess the development of each child they care for to determine if she is meeting all developmental milestones. Teachers need to establish their classrooms as a safe place where families feel loved and encouraged. The early childhood teacher is often a Renaissance person. Teachers who work with older students specialize in certain content, but early childhood educators must be special-education teachers, nurses, musicians, PE teachers, and scientists. While all of this in-depth learning is occurring, an early childhood educator will hold a two-year-old in her arms and gently rock her to sleep.

With this vast array of job requirements, it seems as though our early childhood specialists would deserve an outstanding salary; however, most make close to minimum wage. They have a daunting job, but most child-care programs cannot afford to increase their salaries and still pay all the program's bills. Most child-care providers do not have benefits such as health insurance. They spend their day with young children who can easily spread germs, but they do not have the financial assistance to pay their own medical bills when they get sick themselves. Many child-care providers take work home and even spend their own money on classroom materials because their programs may not have funding for individual classroom budgets. They easily work more than full-time hours with significantly low compensation. It is easy to see why so many child-care providers are leaving the field and not returning.

Compare the job of a child-care provider to that of a public school kindergarten teacher. Both care for a group of young students who need constant supervision. Both must help children learn about their letters and numbers. Both have to create specialized learning strategies for each child in the classroom. Both teach children how to be independent and how to play well with others. Yet, the kindergarten teacher typically makes at least double the salary of the child-care provider. Plus, the public school teacher has medical insurance, paid leave, and a retirement account. This discrepancy is huge!

Child-care programs must maintain a certain level of enrollment at all times in order to pay all of their necessary bills. This means that when enrollment dips, teachers may be laid off to compensate for the lack of income. When enrollment temporarily increases, new teachers must be found and trained in an efficient manner, because all states require a minimum adult-to-child ratio in child-care programs to maintain supervision and safety. This constant balancing act is difficult to maintain, and it is one of the greatest challenges for our centers. As this complicated dance continues and child-care programs teeter on the edge of closure, society must remember that we cannot have a successful economy without stable child care.

THE COVID-19 CRISIS

On March 11, 2020, the World Health Organization announced that the Novel Coronavirus Disease, COVID-19, was officially a pandemic, and on March 13, 2020, the United States was declared to be in a state of emergency. Although the most up-to-date information was constantly changing as the world learned more about this new illness, the Centers for Disease Control and Prevention (CDC) described a list of symptoms including fever, cough, shortness of breath, fatigue, muscle aches, headaches, loss of taste or smell, sore throat, congestion or runny nose, nausea or vomiting, and/or diarrhea (CDC, 2020c). Although many of the symptoms were similar to those of the influenza virus, the death rate for COVID-19 infections was higher than that of the flu (Johns Hopkins Medicine, 2020). Those most at risk to catch the coronavirus included individuals who were sixty years of age or older and individuals with pre-existing medical conditions, such as obesity, asthma, diabetes, and heart disease (CDC, 2020b). Despite the risk factors, people of all ages and backgrounds were contracting the illness. The virus was predominantly spread from person to person by coughing, sneezing, and even talking.

Due to the nature of the disease and the way it was spread, states began to close businesses and limit events where large numbers of people gathered in close spaces. Many states took an in-depth look at businesses such as nursing homes, schools, and child-care programs. Some states mandated that child-care programs close, with minimal sites allowed to stay open for emergency care. Other states limited the types of families who centers were allowed to serve to those of essential employees, medical staff, and first responders. This allowed the centers to choose whether they wanted to remain open. Regardless of which approach was taken, a significant number of the nation's child-care programs had to close, and very few centers had income.

The initial assumption of many Americans was that these closures would be for a minimal amount of time, perhaps two to three weeks. Some centers chose to continue charging families tuition, or a reduced amount of tuition, to cover their costs; however, as the closures continued, it was obvious that this was going to be a lengthy process. State administrators reached out to federal liaisons and asked permission to continue paying child-care programs the cost of tuition for the children who had received a child-care subsidy. This would at least allow programs to have some income to pay their fixed expenses. The federal Office of Child Care approved these requests; however, children on child-care subsidy represent only a small portion of the children in child care throughout the nation. The vast majority of child-care funding in the United States comes from American families, and as the impact of the pandemic set in across the country, many families were uncertain of their financial situations.

In March 2020, the National Association for the Education of Young Children (NAEYC) conducted a national survey of 6,000 child-care providers, asking them how these closures would affect their businesses. Thirty percent of programs surveyed responded that they believed their child-care program would not survive a closure of more than two to three weeks; an additional 16 percent said they could not survive a closure of longer than a month (NAEYC, 2020). Only 11 percent of programs nationwide were not afraid of having to close their businesses without additional federal assistance throughout the pandemic (NAEYC, 2020).

During the time period that most states closed down their child-care programs, child-care providers still had fixed expenses and salaries to consider. With the federal government's expansion of the unemployment system, many programs laid off their staff members with the hope that the employees would be able to support themselves on unemployment payments. The federal government released the Coronavirus Aid, Relief, and Economic Security (CARES) Act (2020) and designated that $3.5 billion specifically go to support child care throughout the United States. Each state and territory was allowed to determine how the funding was distributed to child-care programs, but all funds were supposed to be spent by September 30, 2021, to make sure that child-care providers would have funding in hand to support center operations. In many states, grants were awarded to child-care programs to help them pay their fixed expenses for a short time; however, the federal funding was merely a short-term solution.

Child-care programs that remained open, both those in homes and those in centers, received a very small amount of revenue, because most businesses across the United States were closed and many families chose to keep their children at home during the pandemic. The CDC established health and safety guidelines for child-care programs that decided to remain open, and these guidelines were very challenging for centers to implement. Of course, all child-care programs were keeping the health of the children and staff as their top priority, but many were trying to find a way to both establish a healthy environment and receive enough income to prevent their centers from closing permanently. Some guidelines, such as additional cleaning and temperature checks throughout the day, were manageable, but some of the restrictions, such as reducing class sizes, had the potential to devastate a program financially.

Child-care programs that remained open also had to collaborate with the department of public health on what to do if a child or staff member tested positive for COVID-19. The individual with the illness had to be quarantined for fourteen days due to the incubation period of the illness, but the child-care programs also had to worry about all the other children and staff who had been exposed to the illness. Local health departments were requiring centers to close down classrooms or entire programs for the fourteen-day incubation period to make sure that the illness was not spreading.

Adults tested positive for more cases than children, so staff members were more at risk than students. Centers could not operate without a minimum number of staff. Child-care programs also had to determine whether to charge families during these quarantine closures. Again, they still faced fixed expenses, even when classrooms or buildings were closed, but many families were facing financial hardships of their own. Staff members were willingly putting themselves at risk by volunteering to work with the young children of emergency personnel during the pandemic, so if a staff member tested positive and had to quarantine, programs still wanted the ability to pay their salaries. This was not always possible, depending on the financial stability of the program.

By May 2020, many states had begun to reopen more businesses, and child-care programs had the opportunity to reopen as well. Even with a state's permission to reopen (or permission to serve a larger variety of families), many child-care programs did not have the ability to do so. Staff members were still at home on unemployment payments, and many staff (particularly those who were most at risk to catch the virus) were scared to come back to work. Even though some families desperately needed child care so that they could return to work, other families were looking for any alternative to group child care because they feared for the health of their children. Most centers did not have the financial ability to reopen with a significantly reduced capacity. Some centers chose to remain closed, and other programs reopened with new families begging them for spots that were not available.

A RISK OF COMPLETE COLLAPSE

It became obvious in every community that child-care programs must get back to regular operations. Families needed child care so they could return to work. Child-care providers needed income; unemployment payments or savings would not last forever. The CARES Act funding had assisted many programs with limited amounts of fixed expenses, but now centers had to try to reopen without additional support, relying on the income generated by their fees. It seemed impossible for many programs to achieve this balance. Additional funding was necessary in every state.

As each state began to reopen its economy, most kept capacity restrictions and additional health requirements on all businesses, from restaurants to law offices to schools. Child-care programs in most states were still following the CDC guidelines, along with other state mandates or recommendations, for programs open during the pandemic. Reduced group sizes were a significant obstacle for centers trying to reopen. States were also mandating a variety of health requirements such as central-ized drop-off and pick-up locations for families, additional cleaning throughout the day, temperature checks for children and staff, and not allowing classrooms of children to interact with other classrooms so as to avoid the spread of the illness.

These additional health requirements required more staff members to care for the children and do the necessary cleaning and health screenings; however, reducing the number of children that can attend the program reduced the amount of the funding that the programs could receive. Basically, staffing costs were increasing while income was decreasing. Centers were losing money just to be open. Centers that were lucky had small savings accounts that they could use to offset their weekly losses, but most child-care centers do not make enough profit to have any type of cash reserve. The first centers that were able to reopen were those that were supported by a hospital, a university, or an established business, such as an on-site child care for an employer. In these cases, the larger business could assist the child-care program with its losses. However, family child-care homes or independent nonprofit busi-nesses were apprehensive about reopening; they were also among the first to show signs of financial loss.

After two to three months of closures, most state governments were suffering economic losses themselves. Many states tried to put together aid packages for unemployment recipients, health-care needs, and other family supports such as housing and food distribution. They also had to increase staffing in departments that assist needy families, and these efforts depleted any surplus funds that states may have previously had. Now all eyes were turning once again to the federal government for assistance.

Controversy for school and child-care programs increased when the American Academy of Pediatrics (AAP) announced a slightly different position than what the CDC had been telling the public for months. The AAP (2020a) stated that it was in the best interest of the children to return to child-care and school as long as specific health precautions were taken. They stated that small group sizes were not as essential as keeping the same groups of children together all day to reduce the spread of the illness and keep the germs within a "family group." The AAP also explained that the risk of the illness was not as great for children as the risk of the loss of overall development resulting from lack of supervision, abuse, malnutrition, and the negative impact to social and emotional development.

By June, many states were now starting to see a plateau or decrease in the number of cases being diagnosed in their area. Businesses were reopening, and there were discussions on how colleges and schools were going to reopen in the fall. After travel bans were lifted in many different states, families started to take advantage of reduced airline and hotel rates to enjoy impromptu summer vacations. These trips were particularly appealing to people after being at home for months with "shelter-in-place" orders. Everyone wanted to return to normal life and enjoy the benefits of seeing friends and family again. However, even though COVID-19 cases were no longer on the rise, they were not gone yet. Physicians were able to see that the COVID-19 virus was not affected by warmer temperatures in the way similar viruses, including the flu, were affected. Beaches and amusement parks had thousands of visitors, and the rate of COVID-19 infections began to rise again in many regions.

This time, the hot spots for outbreaks seemed to be focused in southern and coastal states, as vacationers flocked to warmer climates. States that had previously reopened their entire economies now had to re-evaluate whether or not their families were safe. States with a surge in outbreaks began requiring residents to wear facial masks when out in public. This practice became somewhat controversial. Many Americans were abiding by the practice, but questions arose regarding masking for young children: How old must a child be to successfully wear a mask throughout the day? In a group setting such as school or child care, is the child at risk of strangulation if another child pulls the mask or if it gets stuck on a piece of furniture while children are playing? How will masking affect young children with disabilities or children with health conditions? Others began to question the safety of teachers returning to school if masking is required and teachers are more at risk due to age and health conditions: How many children should be in a classroom to keep a healthy environment and support learning? What would happen if children lost another year of face-to-face instruction in elementary and secondary school? How would families adapt if the public school system, a major source of child care, did not open?

As July rolled around, more states began to announce a hybrid learning system, in which students would attend in-person classes for two to three days per week and online classes for the rest of the week; other districts and states planned for another year of virtual learning. Child-care programs across the United States had now sustained more than four months of no income or reduced income and were more at risk than ever for permanently closing.

If elementary students were not going to be in school during the day, where would they go so that they could be safe while parents were at work? Child-care programs that were already open with reduced capacity did not have any additional spaces to serve the influx of elementary students who would need daytime care. The entire system had reached the point of collapse.

CRITICAL QUESTIONS

During a 2020 NAEYC round-table discussion with Child Care and Development Block Grant (CCDBG) state administrators, Commissioner Beth Bye of Connecticut's Office of Early Childhood stated, "The off-ramp for closing early childhood education at the beginning of the pandemic was very quick. It only took a few weeks for programs to close down—less in some states. What we need to realize is that the on-ramp for states to successfully reopen their early childhood programs is going to be much longer." It could easily take a year to eighteen months to be in a place where our programs are able to stand on their own again. We need to give them a great deal of support.

Child-care programs were not operating successfully before the COVID-19 pandemic. The pandemic laid bare both the necessity and the fragile structure of child care in the United States. Child care is absolutely essential to the US economy, and the previous business model that we have been using is unsustainable. The nation must start brainstorming ways to create a child-care system that is reliable enough to support our families. In order to find solutions, there are several essential questions that we must examine:

- Can child-care programs generate enough income to pay their bills and their staff?

- What funding streams support child care, and where do they come from?

- How do we provide child care for all working families, regardless of the type of jobs they have or the hours that they need care?

- Do families know what to look for when they are seeking safe and regulated child care?

- Can we continue to attract teachers to this field without providing a living wage and benefits?

- How do child-care programs support children and families with special needs?

- How do the public school system and the child-care industry partner to make sure that children have the care that they need?

- Has the shift to working at home altered the needs for child care? Is this a temporary change, or will it have an impact in the long term?

Families are apprehensive about returning to child care, due to both the COVID-19 virus and to the decreased capacity to serve the families who need care; however, these are short-term issues. In the long term, child care must be readily available so that the economy can return to full strength.

The human-services industry has focused on looking at the number of children and families who are affected at any point in time by the funding provided. So, if the United States wants to invest in child care, it needs to know the exact numbers of the children who are being helped with that funding. Financial supports and bailouts for other industries, however, do not work in the same manner. When the US government has had to offer financial bailout funds to the airline industry, for example, the approach was significantly different. The overall goal was just to keep America's planes flying. It did not matter if there were more empty seats than full seats at the beginning of the bailout because the overall goal was to make sure that the airlines were still there six months, twelve months, and five years down the road. The airline industry needs to be stable in the future, so the country offers support now, knowing that it will be there when we need it again.

America needs to look at the child-care industry with the same model as that used for bailouts for other industries. We need to make sure that all child-care programs successfully reopen now, because in the long term we are going to need each and every program in order to have a successful economy. Centers are not going to be full in the short term because families and staff members are apprehensive about re-entry. However, if we wait to address this problem until families feel confident in group child care again, there will not be an industry left to save. Child care needs our attention now so that it can be there for our families in the future.

Let's examine the child-care industry and consider the essential questions we must answer.

Chapter 1:
The Cost of Quality

Success in running a child-care program is elusive. Child-care programs are required to follow a minimum set of standards in each state to protect the basic health and safety of the children in attendance. To attract consumers and offer the best program possible, each center attempts to increase the quality of its program while still remaining financially viable. Most child-care programs are established as nonprofit businesses for a reason: it is difficult to meet the bottom line. For-profit programs are still fragile businesses that can begin to deteriorate very quickly.

A child-care program is essentially a school that focuses on children from the time they are born through preschool, or even through elementary school if the program offers after-school care or summer programs. Unlike a typical public school, the child-care program is also a small business. The program must market itself to families, vie with local competition, create policies, and develop an education environment that motivates families to enroll. Like a public school, a child-care program must meet minimum state standards, but beyond those basic requirements the child-care business can decide how to operate. The business determines tuition rates, which families to enroll, and what types of services to offer.

Child-care programs are unique in another aspect. Most states have limited requirements for who can be an administrator in a child-care program; the requirements can be as minimal as a high-school diploma (or a GED) and initial training in the field of early childhood education. This often means that the program director has little to no business training. In many child-care programs, the most skilled classroom teacher is often promoted to the roll of assistant director and eventually director.

The new director cares deeply for the children and can mentor the teachers, but he may have no training on budgets, staff evaluations, or liability insurance. This often makes the small business much more vulnerable to legal or financial challenges.

Child-care programs face other challenges that have nothing to do with the centers' individual management. Throughout the United States, child-care programs receive little state or federal subsidies. The predominant source of funding is the tuition provided by families. This means that working families must provide the money for all of a center's salaries, rent or mortgage payments, utility bills, insurance payments, and food and other consumables. Depending on the number of children enrolled in a program, tuition can be a large expense for each family to provide. To offset that cost, staff members typically receive extremely low salaries. Child-care administrators must balance the program quality with the amount of funding they are able to bring in each month. Tuition must be low enough to attract interested families while still being high enough to cover all the expenses. This balancing act is the reason that child-care programs have such a difficult time providing quality care and remaining successful businesses.

COST VERSUS QUALITY: BUSINESSES ON THE MARGIN

One of the first items to consider when looking at the fragile structure of a child-care program is the difference between price and cost. *Cost* refers to the expenses a program incurs for taking care of an individual child plus the added expenses of maintaining and running the facility. For example, the cost of caring for a two-year-old child would include not only the salaries for the staff members, but also a proportion of all facility expenses, such as the electricity and other utility bills, the food the child consumes during the day, cleaning supplies used in the classroom, and any other materials the program must pay for to take care of the child.

According to the annual report from Child Care Aware of America (2019), the Center for American Progress estimates that the average cost of caring for an infant is approximately $14,000 per year, assuming that the family provides the diapering supplies and all the formula. Despite the cost of care for an infant, the annual price associated with infant care is between $8,000 and $12,000 per year (Workman and Jessen-Howard, 2018). That's right: child-care providers are not actually charging the full cost of care. One reason for this is that parents cannot afford the full cost. If a child-care program were to charge $14,000 for a year of care, the average monthly charge would be approximately $1,167. Many families cannot cover that expense, particularly if they have more than one child in care at the same time. This means that child-care providers lose money by operating most infant classrooms; yet, they continue to keep their infant classrooms open. Why?

When a child starts in a child-care program as an infant and the family has a positive experience, the family is more likely to stay at the same center until the child ages out of care. Loyalty is created between the family and the provider. Another reason is that, although the infant classroom (and even the toddler classroom) causes the center to lose money, the child-care provider anticipates covering that loss with the tuition received from the preschool and school-age enrollments. An infant classroom may have only six to ten children, but preschool and school-age programs can have twenty to thirty children enrolled at once. This is why you will rarely see a child-care program that only serves infants and toddlers. There is no way to make up that loss without charging an exorbitant fee to the families.

To stay in business, centers must serve infants and toddlers as well as preschoolers. According to research done by the Center for American Progress (Workman and Jessen-Howard, 2019), infant and toddler care is 61 percent more expensive to operate than preschool care. With this delicate balance in play, child-care programs can have a difficult time staying open if their infant and toddler classrooms are full and their preschool classroom enrollment is low.

It can also be more difficult for smaller child-care programs to meet their bottom line in comparison to larger center-based care (Workman and Jessen-Howard, 2019). A center that has only twenty slots will face significantly smaller staffing requirements and fewer facility costs; however, each child's tuition is a much larger percentage of the overall income. If the program has two empty slots in the preschool class-room—representing 10 percent of the overall income—that can have a devastating effect. In comparison, for a larger program that enrolls up to two hundred children, two empty slots represent 1 percent of the overall income. Although there are larger costs associated with operating a business of that size, a 1 percent income loss can have a much smaller effect on an operation.

A MODEL FOR FINANCIAL STABILITY

Louise Stoney, an early childhood–finance expert, has done significant research on the cost of quality for early childhood education programs. Based on her research, she has developed a financial model called "The Iron Triangle" to show how early childhood programs can remain financially stable (Stoney, 2010). The three signifi-cant pillars of the triangle consist of full enrollment, full fee collection, and revenues that cover per-child cost. Most often, child-care programs focus on full enrollment: If each available slot in the program is full, then administrators assume that the child-care program will succeed financially. However, when child-care programs are administered by teachers without business training, it is often the other two pillars that cause programs to be the most vulnerable.

Child-care programs typically set their rates to be competitive with the local market; however, if tuition does not cover the per-child cost, the shortfall will eventually catch up to the program. For example, in the situation previously discussed in which the infant rate for care is significantly higher than the preschool rate, the program can lose money when the preschool classroom is not fully enrolled. However, if the price of the infant care matches the amount that it costs to care for a very young child, then the center will be more financially stable when the program is not at full capacity. If the combination of parent tuition and any potential government subsidy for low-income families will not cover the cost of child care, then the program needs to find other sources of income, such as donations, grants, or in-kind support.

Another potential financial risk for child-care programs is uncollected income. This is an area that is often challenging for child-care providers because their top priority is caring for the children and families. It may seem harsh to constantly remind families to pay tuition in a timely manner; however, child-care directors must remember that lack of income can jeopardize their ability to care for all the families in the program.

Since child care can be the largest budget expense for families with young children, once a family gets one or two weeks behind on tuition, it can be very challenging to catch up on payments. When a child-care program continues to allow a family to attend while accumulating debt, the past-due amount can grow quickly. All states have a child-care subsidy program through which families can apply for support based on income. If a family does not qualify for a subsidy, the child-care program must determine how to assist them in paying the expected fees. Some centers find a potential donor or foundation that is willing to cover the fees for families struggling with the cost of care. Other centers reserve a small number of child-care slots (above the required capacity for full enrollment) that they can offer to families who lack the ability to pay tuition.

However, if the center is counting on the tuition to make its budget, then it is essential to have a policy in place to handle what could potentially be a very emotional process. A growing number of centers use automatic billing to strengthen their ability to collect fees. Some child-care centers have established policies on how far behind a family can fall on tuition before sacrificing their spot in the program. If the center budget allows, it may be helpful to have a business manager who handles most of the tuition matters and policies related to payment, so that the director can focus time and attention on the families.

QUALITY = DECREASING INCOME AND INCREASING COSTS

In a study conducted in 2017, the Prichard Committee for Academic Excellence specifically looked at the cost of quality child care in the Commonwealth of Kentucky. To put a price on quality child care, the advocacy organization first had to define *quality child care*. Along with all the basic health and safety requirements required by the state, the Prichard Committee found that an increase of quality learning interactions in the early childhood classroom requires more teacher training, smaller classroom sizes, and an increase in salaries for the teachers in the classrooms. They also found that quality classrooms for children with special needs include smaller classroom sizes and support from specialists in the field of disabilities (Prichard Committee for Academic Excellence, 2017).

These findings are similar to other requirements for high-quality early childhood education programs. One of the highest accreditations that any early childhood education program can obtain in the United States is that offered by NAEYC. NAEYC's accreditation process evaluates programs in several different areas: relationships, curriculum, teaching, assessment of child progress, health, staff competencies, preparation and support, families, community relationships, physical environment, and management and leadership. Within the subcategories of the accreditation process, programs are challenged to provide significant training to staff members, reduce group sizes in classrooms to allow teachers to spend more time with each student, and assess the individual learning needs of all the children involved in the program. Each of these quality improvements has an effect on the finances of the program.

Many states also have a statewide quality rating scale in place. Instead of a single level of accreditation like NAEYC's, states such as North Carolina use a multilevel system that rates programs from the minimum level requirements (one star) up to the highest level of care (five stars). To achieve the five-star rating in the state, child-care programs must decrease the staff-to-child ratio, provide further training to staff members, and offer benefits to staff such as higher wage incentives and medical insurance.

Whether centers look at a national or local option for accreditation, the overall structure requires them to take fewer children into their programs and to spend more money on staffing, training, and materials. This type of environment does attract more qualified staff members, and the staff is more likely to stay at the facility longer if they are well taken care of and have a smaller group of students. Parents are more likely to enroll in a program that provides small groups and more learning activities for their children. The biggest question that the management of the program must ask is, "Can the program bring in enough revenue to support the staff and the curriculum demands?"

High-quality child-care programs can charge more than other programs. In North Carolina, a five-star program typically costs more than a two-star program. It is also possible for child-care programs to price themselves out of the market. If a program is far too expensive for a family to afford, then it doesn't matter to the family that the group sizes are smaller. They have to consider other programs with fewer amenities because they only have a certain amount of money each month to spend on child care. Many programs try to operate in the mid-range of quality. They want to be above the minimum requirements for the state, but they do not want to be so expensive that families cannot afford to attend. This means that many children do not have access to the highest quality care because child-care programs cannot afford to offer it.

The child-care subsidy program in each state has the goal of helping low-wage families place their children in high-quality child care; however, the subsidy rate in most states will not cover the full cost of care. To set the rate of subsidy it offers, each state surveys the cost of child care at every program to learn the average cost of care for the state as a whole, for each region in the state, and for the age of the child in care. Once the market rate is established, the state can then determine how much reimbursement can be issued. For example, perhaps the state can afford to pay up to the fiftieth percentile in reimbursement. That would mean that the state would cover the full cost of care for 50 percent of the child-care programs in the state. However, if a family receiving the subsidy decided to attend one of the more expensive programs, then the state would not be able to cover the full cost, and the family would have to pay the difference in cost over the subsidy rate. Typically, the highest quality programs have an overage above the state subsidy rate. If a family found a high-quality program that cost $225 per week, and the state subsidy only covered $160 per week, the family would be responsible for $65 per week. That would add up with a total overage cost of $260 per month. For a family that is already struggling to pay essential bills, $260 per month is a huge expense. If the family could not afford the $260 per-month fee, they would need to look for a less expensive child-care program, and most likely, the program would also offer less quality.

Because the market rate is significantly higher for infant and toddler care than for preschool care, families on a subsidy may need to find an even lower-quality infant and toddler program to avoid overages they cannot afford. (This is especially problematic because a child this age is at his most vulnerable and is just establishing essential relationships.)

Young children living in poverty are already more likely to start elementary school academically behind students living above the federal poverty level. This discrepancy in child care makes it even more challenging for all students to enter kindergarten ready to learn.

STAFF TURNOVER

A high staff turnover rate can dramatically affect the quality of a child-care program, and it can be one of the biggest challenges of managing an early childhood center. Staff turnover usually occurs when an early childhood educator leaves one program for a different one. Large numbers of staff members in early childhood programs also leave the field completely to go to higher-paying positions outside early care and education. Staff members leave an early childhood position for many different reasons, including low wages, lack of medical benefits, unskilled coworkers, poor working relationships with supervisors, the economic instability of the program, and lack of sufficient training to do the job (McLean, 2020). Less common reasons to leave include moving out of the city or state, commute time, career change, going back to school, or deciding to stay home with a child instead of working.

Most child-care providers understand the job requirements when they accept a position. They know they will receive lower wages than in many other positions, but they also enjoy working with children. They often stay in low-paying positions because they develop significant bonds with the children they care for each day. At the same time, many child-care providers have their own children to care for. Low wages can sometimes be offset by reduced-cost child care for a provider's children, which can be a significant benefit. Once their children grow up and no longer need enrollment in the child-care program, however, it may be harder to keep those staff members at the facility.

Child-care providers who make so little above minimum wage will often switch to working at another child-care program for as little as a twenty-cents-per-hour wage increase. A change is not inconceivable when the previous job offered the child-care provider so very little. Centers generally are not making huge profits and withholding that money from the staff; they simply cannot afford to pay more.

A child-care provider's decision to leave a center can have a big impact on the program. First, it can take a child-care program weeks, even months, to replace a care provider. The nation is currently facing a staffing crisis in child-care programs due to low wages and high expectations. When a center posts an available position, there are usually not a huge number of qualified applicants (McLean, 2020). Once the program director begins screening potential candidates, conducting interviews, checking references, and completing mandatory background checks can take a significant amount of time.

During this period, the classroom is missing a staff member, and other members of the staff must take turns stepping in to meet the required adult-to-child ratios. A temporary staff member does not know the children well, so the children may be apprehensive to interact with the new adult. The newest teacher may not know the best way to put each child to sleep, how to entertain the children during a diaper change, or how to calm a child down in the morning when a parent leaves for work. The parents notice the additional stress on the children, and they often put pressure on the director to hire a new teacher quickly. They may even demand that the director find a way to bring back the previous teacher. Other parents who are more devoted to the teacher than to the child-care program may transfer their children to the teacher's new center; the director ends up losing paying customers during the transition.

Once a new staff member is hired, he or she is still not ready to enter the classroom immediately. The staff member must complete new-hire paperwork and orientation training in the new child-care program. New staff must read all the center's policies and agree to follow them while employed at the program. While the new team member is being trained, staffing is still low, so the director may need to assist in the classroom during this time instead of completing management tasks. The director also needs to make sure that all of the parents in the classroom meet the new staff member and feel comfortable with the teacher before leaving their children alone with him or her for the first time. Once all the paperwork and required training is completed, the new employee can finally begin to fill the position that he or she was hired to do.

An immense amount of time and resources is used in the period from a teacher's resignation until a new teacher begins in the classroom. Stress levels increase for the children, the parents, the director, and the existing staff members. Children have to start from the beginning, creating a relationship with the new teacher. This is why staff turnover can be devastating to a program. Further, the possibility always exists that the new employee will not be a good fit, and the staffing process will start over much more quickly than is beneficial for the children or the program.

One study on child care in Mississippi showed that constant staff turnover in child care can put children at significant risk (Butrymowicz and Mader, 2016). With constant turnover, many administrators are scrambling just to keep the required number of staff members in the classrooms. When untrained staff members begin working with young children, they often do not have the skills needed to be successful at their jobs. High turnover and lack of proper training can lead to staff yelling at the children, corporal punishment, improper administration of first aid, and unsafe sleeping practices for infants (Butrymowicz and Mader, 2016). All these dangerous practices can easily be reduced with consistent staffing and quality training plans. Directors in the Mississippi study all agreed that they were willing to fire a staff member who mistreats a child, but they also expressed concern about the best methods to keep talented staff members at their programs when they don't have the ability to pay more.

Higher-quality centers can avoid this process somewhat by paying higher wages and encouraging staff with smaller classroom sizes. Other child-care programs may continually be going through the staffing process, which can take a great deal of time and attention away from the children. As Butrymowicz and Mader write in their 2016 report, "High turnover and low pay for employees may undermine the state's child care system." If turnover is one of the key issues that degrades child-care program quality, then how can child-care programs address it without charging rates that are impossible for parents to pay?

TWO DIFFERENT PERSPECTIVES: JESSICA AND ELIZA

Different types of child-care programs can meet the needs of a community. Communities with a great deal of poverty may benefit from a Head Start or Early Head Start program that focuses on making sure that every child, even the most vulnerable, is ready for kindergarten. Communities with a great deal of commerce may have businesses that offer on-site child care for their employees to make sure that employees can attend work regularly and stay focused on their work instead of worrying about their young children. Many communities have independent child-care programs that are open to anyone in the community who can pay the fee, as long as spots are available. Each of these types of child care have a place in a community, and each type also has its own set of requirements to operate the business effectively.

An on-site child-care program devoted to working with one business must make sure that there is enough demand for child care to reach full enrollment. But, the program does benefit from having the sponsoring business do the marketing for the child-care program. An independent child-care program, on the other hand, can serve a variety of families in the community, but it must make sure that the services it offers and the costs are equitable to the needs of the community.

Jessica is the director and owner of a child-care program that she started in a rural area of her state. Eliza is the director of a child-care program on-site at one of the largest hospitals in the state, and she serves only the staff from the hospital in her program. Both directors started off as teachers in the field of early childhood education, and they learned many of the skills to be a successful director while in the position. Their job responsibilities primarily include staff scheduling, hiring, parent tours, enrolling new families, maintaining staff and child files, occasionally assisting in classrooms when they are needed, communicating with parents, maintaining the program waiting list, supervising the budget, ordering supplies, and addressing concerns of staff or parents. Eliza reports to a supervisor at the hospital; Jessica owns her own business, so she has more freedom to supervise her own program.

The traditional job responsibilities take about 75 percent of their work time; the rest of their time is occupied by details that they did not expect when they started their positions as directors. Those other jobs can include everything from unclogging toilets to meeting with parents who need advice on a toddler who bites. Customer service is a full-time part of the positions because both child-care programs are small businesses and families are free to choose to send their children to a different program. To make families feel as comfortable as possible, Jessica and Eliza are always available to assist families when they are at work (and sometimes outside of business hours).

Each director has a master's degree in her field and is well educated on how to run a high-quality child-care program. Both of their child-care programs are accredited. Eliza's program has a four-star rating out of the potential five stars that her state offers, and Jessica's program has a five-star rating and NAEYC accreditation. Despite all the accolades, one program is significantly more financially stable than the other. Due to the connection between Eliza's child-care program and the hospital, she enjoys a safety net for her center that Jessica can only dream about.

Jessica opened her child-care center in 1999 after a year of creating a business plan and surveying the needs of the community. Opening her child-care program is a way for her to serve the families in her area, and her mission is to love and serve the children that come into her program. Despite her experience and her education and the top credentials of her program, Jessica can afford to pay herself only $20,000 per year. Her child-care program is obviously not her family's main source of income. With that type of budget for management of the program, she does not have the funding to hire an assistant director or a bookkeeper. She is responsible for all management tasks and must often work evenings and on weekends.

Jessica's program typically has some annual staff turnover. She is located close to a university and hires college students each year. She is able to pay closer to entry-level wages, and students are often willing to stay with her program while completing a degree. She does not have the ability to offer health insurance to her employees; however, many of her younger staff members are still able to be on their parents' health-insurance plans. Jessica does cover the cost of background checks, tuberculosis skin tests, online training, and uniform T-shirts for her employees. She also allows each new employee to spend a week shadowing experienced staff members before working on their own. This is a great training advantage for the staff, but it is a financial loss to her for the first week of the staff member's employment. Jessica also works hard to purchase all the supplies that her teachers need for classroom activities.

Jessica's program is an amazing asset to her community, but she and her staff members are definitely underpaid for their hard work. Like many small-business owners, Jessica never gets to stop working. Because she has chosen to obtain such high program credentials, she is operating with lower income and greater expenses. She is able to meet her bills because she pays herself so little, yet one disaster, such as the COVID-19 pandemic, can have a devastating effect on a program that does so much good for many families.

Eliza's situation is much different than Jessica's situation. Because her child-care program is located on the hospital site, Eliza does not have to worry about many facility costs. The hospital is involved in the budget and uses the child-care program as a benefit to their employees, so Eliza has enough funding to pay an assistant director and an office manager. This administrative support gives her the opportunity to work a forty-hour work week from time to time. As the primary administrator, there are always reasons that she will work additional hours, but she can leave responsible staff members in charge when she wants to be away from the office.

Another benefit for Eliza's program is that her staff enjoy one of the highest pay rates in her town. Since they technically work with the hospital, they also receive excellent medical insurance. With this type of compensation, along with being a highly accredited child-care program, Eliza has very limited staff turnover. She also is able to pay for staff background checks, tuberculosis skin tests, and mandatory training. When staff make purchases for their classrooms, she is able to reimburse them.

Eliza still has a budget to maintain, and she is held accountable to the hospital for her purchases and her staffing choices. However, the hospital can afford to pay her a salary that matches her level of education and management skills. In months when Eliza does not meet her anticipated budget, she typically tries to adjust the budget in the following month. Because Eliza's program has a consistent waiting list, she can maintain full enrollment without difficulty.

With enrollment at capacity, monthly budget variations are usually not significant. Of course, the COVID-19 pandemic affected all child-care programs significantly, even if they were financially stable prior to the pandemic. The greatest advantage for Eliza's program was that, when the center suffered a significant financial loss while most families were sheltering in place at home, the hospital was able to support the child-care program and help it sort through the difficulty created by the pandemic. Of course, the hospital suffered losses as well. Both the hospital and the child-care program had to furlough some staff members to adjust to the quarantine, but both organizations were able to come through the time-off loss. Independent programs, such as Jessica's, do not have the same ability to recover.

Jessica's and Eliza's child-care programs are both essential. They are high-quality programs that serve large numbers of children in their communities. Although not their primary market, they serve families who use child-care subsidies, so they both provide child-care access to a variety of families. The child-care system is not set up to support Jessica's program in a way that guarantees its stability, however. This is a critical flaw in the system.

Chapter 2:
Achieving a Living Wage

Child-care providers are paid what we can afford to pay them, not what they deserve (Butrymowicz and Mader, 2016). Despite the fact that society is not treating child-care providers like a valuable commodity, they are desperately needed. There are approximately 15 million children in the United States under the age of six years whose parents are both in the workforce (Thomason et al., 2018). Six million of those children have parents working in low-wage jobs and are more at risk for entering kindergarten at a developmental rate below their peers. If 65 percent of families with young children must have all parents in the workforce, then child-care providers are needed to stand in the gap. Parents need child-care providers to keep their children safe and healthy while the parents are working. Children need child-care providers so they feel secure and loved while they are away from their families. The community needs these providers to prepare children for kindergarten so that they have the best opportunity to be successful in the future.

When you read the job description, the decision to be a child-care provider seems overwhelming. The provider must play the roles of educator, medical professional, nutritionist, janitor, special educator, manual-labor specialist, and parent. With a list of so many skills accumulated on one résumé, it would be easy to assume that child-care providers are well compensated. The truth is that most child-care providers work hours beyond their minimum requirements and struggle financially to feed their own families. Many leave the field completely at some point in their careers because the medical, physical, and financial burdens of their positions are too heavy for their families to bear. In order to begin to fully understand the essential role of the child-care provider, society must understand both the demands of the job and the effects of the lack of appropriate compensation.

HIGH JOB EXPECTATIONS

When child-care programs were initially established in the early nineteenth century, the goal was for parents to leave their child at a program for safety reasons. As knowledge of child development grew, educators began to understand the importance of giving children a quality environment at a young age. The expectation for child care shifted from a safe babysitting environment to an early education classroom for children as young as infants. The job description of early child-care providers also began to change. At one point, a child-care provider simply needed to enjoy being around children. But today, the preferred list of qualifications can include a degree in the field of early childhood education; additional training hours, including on how to conduct developmental assessments; experience working in a child-care program, writing lesson plans, and working with children who have special needs; a medical release stating that the candidate is capable of the required job duties; and a clean background check.

A nationwide staff crisis in the field of early education has prevented many child-care programs from hiring employees with the desired education and experience. Many centers have taken the approach of hiring teachers who are recent high-school or college graduates pursuing their first professional position. The child-care programs then train these apprentice teachers themselves to develop the skills and work ethic they prefer in their staff members. Once the program has established that the candidate's health allows her to complete the job duties and that the criminal background checks show no concerns, program directors can train their new staff members to perform a long list of professional skills.

The foundation of child care is protecting the health and safety of the children, so the first duty of the providers is to supervise the children at all times. This means that the teacher must always be able to see each child in the classroom. Early educators must learn how to place themselves in the classroom so that they can view every child. It also means that child-care providers never have the opportunity to take a break while working. Of course, child-care staff will get their mandatory meal breaks, but when the provider is in the classroom, she must always be aware. There is never an opportunity to sit down and rest without paying attention to the job responsibilities. On the playground, child-care providers must move around to keep an eye on all the children instead of sitting to take a rest. Child-care providers must always be engaged with the children instead of having in-depth conversations with a coworker. The children are always the top responsibility, a philosophy that can prevent many injuries.

Early educators must also work hard to prevent the spread of illness in the classroom. They must be diligent about cleaning surfaces and toys where germs may lurk. They must assist young children who are just learning to turn away from others to cough, sneeze into a tissue, and wash their own hands. Teachers must be adamant about following hygienic routines for diaper changes. Also, early childhood educators must learn about common childhood illnesses and be able to identify the symptoms so they can assist families with pursuing medical care quickly when a child is symptomatic. When an emergency occurs, the child-care provider must also be skilled at administering first aid.

Once a child-care provider learns how to keep children healthy and safe, she then needs to learn about how each child develops. To plan fun and educational activities, the educator must know what the children are capable of doing at each milestone. It is crucial to learn about children with special needs and how a diagnosis may affect a child's ability to develop. Once the teacher begins to understand these skills, then she can begin to create lesson plans to carry out in the classroom each week. Lesson plans should include activities that promote language development, motor skills, independence skills, and pre-academic skills such as emerging literacy and pre-math.

Along with lesson plans, early childhood educators must learn about documentation. Child-care providers need to document details about each child's development, interests, and the skills being mastered. This will help with lesson planning, but it is also very important information to share with parents and the teacher in next year's classroom. Documentation can provide essential information for a parent to share with a doctor if a child becomes sick or if the parent has concerns about a child's behavior or development.

Child-care providers help children meet their basic needs each day by serving healthy meals and helping children rest when necessary. Providers must also develop a strong relationship with the children's families so that they can both feel comfortable expressing concerns and asking questions of each other. Of course, the child-care provider must establish a strong relationship with the child. The child needs to feel safe with the provider in order to learn and grow when the parents are away. The child also needs to feel the love and support of the child-care provider throughout the day.

Considering that a child-care provider could be in a room of eight infants or a classroom of up to twenty-five preschoolers, this is a long list of skills that the provider must master and work hard to achieve. The provider must have support from the program director and coworkers to be able to fulfill all these responsibilities. To devote herself so purposefully to a job of this magnitude, it is essential for the child-care provider to feel support from the child-care program and from the families. But it is very hard to feel supported when the provider is worried about her ability to pay bills and support her own family.

LOW WAGES AND FEW BENEFITS

Looking at the financial picture of the child-care provider can be a distressing view. Research shows that there are approximately two million child-care providers working across the United States (Gould, 2015). Although a large number of these providers work in child-care centers or preschools, many provide home-based care in their own residences or in the homes of the children. Fifty-five percent of America's child-care providers are between the ages of twenty-three and forty-nine years of age, so many of these providers are working while also raising their own families (Gould, 2015).

Other research shows us essential demographics that the community should keep in mind:

- Ninety-four percent of child-care providers in the United States are women.

- Forty percent of child-care providers are people of color, mostly women of color.

- More than half (52 percent) of the child-care providers in the United States are also mothers (Child Care Aware of America, 2019).

This is a group of individuals who highly value young children, so it is not unusual to think that many of them are supporting their own families.

Many of the job responsibilities listed for a child-care provider are extremely similar to those of a kindergarten teacher. Both teachers sing songs and dance with their students. Both teachers lead large- and small-group activities to help their students learn to count and identify alphabet letters. Both teachers help children to stop crying when they are dropped off at school and to become more independent in the bathroom. There is one significant difference, though. The national average income for a child-care provider—approximately $25,000 per year—is half the median income of a kindergarten teacher in a K-12 school system (Child Care Aware of America, 2019). The public school system typically has a higher requirement for minimum education than most private child-care programs; however, 35 percent of providers who work in a child-care center have a four-year degree and are still paid a very low wage for the work they do with young children (Thomason et al., 2018).

Child-care providers who offer home-based child care are typically paid even less, though they offer essential services, such as child care at night and on weekends, that child-care centers may not provide. The average hourly wage for a family child-care home provider (who acts as both a teacher and an administrator) is $10 per hour (Child Care Aware of America, 2019). When providers care for children in their homes, it is typically not a forty-hour work week. Most in-home child-care providers work with children an average of fifty-four hours per week (Child Care Aware of America, 2019). Because these child-care providers also must fill an administrative role, they typically spend an additional fifteen to sixteen hours per week on unpaid administrative work.

Along with paying lower wages, most financially vulnerable child-care programs are not able to offer child-care providers a benefits package to supplement their salaries. Many programs strive to offer paid time off to their employees for vacation and sick time, but they may be able to offer that type of benefit only to full-time employees, not to all staff members. Insurance is an expensive benefit that most child-care programs can only dream of offering their employees. Only 15 percent of child-care providers receive medical insurance from their employer (Child Care Aware of America, 2019). This can be very challenging for child-care providers who do not have an option for obtaining health insurance through another family member. Working with a classroom of young children each day exposes child-care providers to many different illnesses. Without health insurance, a trip to the doctor and an antibiotic can easily cost $200. Many child-care providers develop strong immunity to illnesses when they work in the field for a number of years, but new employees frequently get sick. The COVID-19 virus was an exception for even veteran child-care staff. Child-care providers put themselves at risk to work with young children of essential employees during the heart of the outbreak, often with no medical coverage to take care of themselves should they contract the virus.

One benefit that many child-care programs can offer their employees is discounted child care for their own children. This is one of the few motivating factors for many young parents to join the field of child care. A large number of child-care providers cannot afford child care for their own children. In thirty-two states, the cost of child care for an infant is more than one-third of the total income of a child-care provider (Gould, 2015). Many young parents have more than one child to provide child care for, and they still need income for their family. When child-care programs offer a significant discount on child care for their employees, it is a huge incentive for staff members to stay at the center. Even if the employees want to consider a position elsewhere, they may not want to disrupt their children's daily routine. When a child-care program offers infant-through-school-age care, it has the potential to encourage employees to stay at the program for a significant amount of time.

TURNOVER: CONSEQUENCES FOR STAFF

Staff turnover has a large impact on child-care programs, but it can have a detrimental effect on individual staff members as well. Low wages in care services almost guarantee high rates of staff turnover (Thomason et al., 2018). It is hard for an employee to stay in a low-paying, challenging work position when she knows that higher-paying positions exist. At the same time, switching jobs has an impact on an employee's entire family.

First, it is critical to acknowledge the effect a job change has on relationships. In an office position, an employee may choose to leave for a higher-paying job, but she may still regret leaving close friends behind. The employee can reach out to former coworkers and maintain those relationships. In a child-care setting, a provider grows extremely close to the children in the classroom. In a way, the provider is a part of the family that is helping the parents raise these children. Should the child-care provider accept a new job to better support her own family, she must separate from the children in her current classroom—not a simple process. It can become even more upsetting when the provider sees how the children may be impacted by the loss of someone they trust.

Every transfer to a new position can also affect the child-care provider's career. Many administrators are apprehensive to hire a child-care provider who has moved frequently to new positions in her past. Child care has a much higher turnover rate than many other professions, so administrators expect to see some of that on a résumé. However, if the potential employee's work history makes it look unlikely that she will stay very long at the child-care program, then a director is more likely to hire someone else to avoid having to start the interview process again in a short amount of time.

Another complication with staff turnover is starting over as a new employee. With each move to a new job, the child-care provider becomes a probationary employee again. The provider must learn a new set of program policies. She may lose any accumulated time off from a past job and have to start over with no leave time at a new position. For child-care providers who are privileged to have health insurance, they can face a gap in their coverage during a job transition. They have no seniority at a new center to request days off. All these side effects to job transitions can have a negative impact on both the new employee and the child-care provider.

A job transition can also negatively affect the child-care provider's family. Switching jobs can cause lots of small changes that require the family to alter their routines. One of the largest changes can be child care for the provider's children. Should the provider switch them to the new program? Will the provider get a discount at the new child-care program, or will having her own children at the center make it harder to complete the job effectively? Do the parents need to change the morning and afternoon drop-off routines to get everyone to school and work on time? Will the job hours be the same? Will a dramatic change in hours affect family meals and extracurricular activities? Each of these changes needs to be considered before switching jobs, even when an increase in income is desperately needed.

GOVERNMENT ASSISTANCE FOR PROVIDERS

Due to chronically low wages offered to child-care providers throughout the United States, a full-time position at a child-care program may not be enough to meet the provider's economic needs. Research conducted by Child Care Aware of America (2019) shows that 36.7 percent of child-care providers live below 200 percent of the federal poverty level (FPL). Of that number, 14.7 percent live *below* the FPL, compared to 6.7 percent of employees in other industries.

Of course, the state that the child-care provider lives in and the cost of living in that state can have a significant impact on the family's financial stability. In rural states, such as Kentucky and Tennessee, 10 percent of providers are unable to pay their bills based on their salaries (Gould, 2015). The story is quite different in urban areas. In Boston, for example, 90 percent of child-care providers are unable to pay their bills based on their salaries (Gould, 2015). These numbers are based on the income needed for one person, so a provider with a larger family may be struggling even more. Despite the range in cost of living, child-care providers are essential in every area throughout the United States.

When a full-time salary is not sufficient to meet their financial needs, child-care providers will look for other options. Some have multiple jobs. Many providers work all day at a child-care program and then care for other children at their home on nights and weekends. Others may find a second job outside the industry. A large portion must turn to federal subsidy programs to meet their basic needs. An estimated 43 percent of child-care providers throughout the United States receive some sort of government assistance (McLean, 2020). This assistance may include the Supplemental Nutrition Assistance Program (SNAP, previously called food stamps), housing assistance, child-care subsidies, and/or Medicaid.

DELIA'S STORY

Although statistics can be motivating, it can be an extremely eye-opening experience to speak to a child-care provider who has dedicated her career to young children and still cannot achieve financial independence. Delia began working in child care in 2006 right after she graduated from high school. Her mother had worked in a child-care program for years as a cook, and Delia had grown up around the program and the employees at the center. Upon graduation, she knew that she needed to get a job to help her mother with their bills. She applied for a position at the child-care program where her mother had worked, and she was offered a job as an assistant teacher in a toddler classroom. The lead teacher in the classroom, Ms. Gladys, had been with the program more than twenty years and was a great mentor. At the same time, Ms. Gladys was having a harder time lifting children and getting up off the floor, so Delia's energy was a help to Ms. Gladys with a lot of the more labor-intensive jobs in the classroom.

When Delia first started working for the program, she made only a little more than minimum wage. At the time, it was not a problem because she was still living with her mother and her new income helped pay their bills. Delia couldn't afford a car, so she rode the bus to work. Because her hours were the same each day, riding the bus usually wasn't a problem, but whenever the director asked her to work an extra shift, she could do so only if the bus schedule worked for her. If the bus was late, so was Delia. Another financial benefit for Delia was that her food costs were low, because she ate breakfast and lunch at the child-care program. As a result, she and her mother needed groceries only for their dinners and weekend meals.

The first year that Delia worked at the child-care program, she got sick several times. The child-care program did offer health insurance, but its cost would take a significant portion out of Delia's paycheck, so she had decided to go without it. After all, she was young and in very good health. Most of the time when she got sick it was just a cold, and she could go to the grocery store to get cold medicine, which usually took care of the problem. Unfortunately, there were two times that first winter that cold medicine did not work. Once, Delia was diagnosed with strep throat, and the other time with bronchitis.

When her throat hurt and she ran a fever in December, and still did not feel better after several days, she decided to go to the local medical clinic. The doctor was very helpful, but the cost of the visit and the price of the medicine came to $150. After that expense, she and her mother could not pay their rent, so Delia had to call several different churches to see if any of them could help. Finally, she found a church that had a special fund to support people with the cost of housing during the winter months.

When Delia got sick again in February, she decided to go to the health department instead of the clinic, thinking it would be much less expensive. She took the bus in the morning, and she let her program director know that she would be a couple of hours late. At lunchtime, still in the waiting room, she called the director again, this time to let her know that she would need to take the entire day off. Because Delia hadn't saved much of her paid time off, she would have to take unpaid leave for the full day. That wasn't a much better alternative to going to the clinic.

As Delia worked at the child-care program longer, many of the families got to know her well. They asked her to come to their homes to babysit, and many of them even picked her up and drove her home afterward. During the holidays, the families at the center gave Delia and her mother wonderful gifts and gift cards as a way to show appreciation. All of these perks were secondary to the fact that Delia loved the children and her coworkers. Her director had encouraged her several times to pursue a degree in early childhood education, but Delia already had the job that she wanted, so that seemed unnecessary.

About four years after Delia had started working at the child-care program, a number of new challenges arose. She was twenty-two years old when she learned that she was unexpectedly pregnant. She had no health insurance and no money to care for a child. She did earn some extra money from babysitting for families at the child-care program, but it was not enough to help support herself and an infant. She realized that she needed a medical card to get prenatal care for herself and the baby. She asked the director for a day off and spent the entire day at the health department to apply for the medical card. The health department also helped her apply for the Women, Infants, and Children (WIC) nutrition program, so that she could eat properly and take vitamins while she was pregnant.

Delia decided to put up flyers at her church and at the child-care program about babysitting so that she could earn extra money for a crib and baby clothes before the baby arrived. She didn't want to tell anyone yet about her pregnancy, but she knew that she would have to tell the director because each visit to the health department could easily take an entire day. The director was very excited for Delia, but she did want her to be careful about how much weight she was lifting in the two-year-old room each day. Ms. Gladys was having a harder and harder time picking up the children, so Delia was doing most of the diaper changes. Lifting ten two-year-olds onto the diaper-changing table was a lot of work for a pregnant woman.

Once Delia finally told her coworkers and the children's parents that she was expecting her first child, everyone went out of their way to support her. Families brought her clothes that their children had outgrown, and staff members all donated money to purchase a crib. It was a huge relief to her that everyone helped her so much, because her pregnancy had very quickly become high risk. Delia's mother had developed hypertension when she was pregnant with Delia, and now Delia was going through the same thing with her baby. The doctor had asked her to reduce her hours at work, but that was not possible because she needed her salary so badly. Instead,

Delia stopped babysitting and came home each evening to relax and follow the doctor's orders.

Delia continue to work full time until she had her son, but the money wasn't enough for all of the new expenses that she now faced. The health department staff talked to her about the child-care subsidy program, and her boss, who had worked with many parents who used that program, helped her apply. The center where Delia worked took children only when they turned two years old, so Delia had to figure out how provide child care for her newborn and still work. Delia's mother had severe asthma, making it more difficult for her to work around the children without getting sick. The director told Delia that there was a limited amount of child-care subsidy for what the state called "family, friend, or neighbor care." Delia qualified for this program. Her mother could apply to provide in-home child care for her grandson and be paid by the state to watch him while Delia continued to work. This seemed like the best solution for their family.

Delia relied heavily on the subsidies that she received from the state. She and her son remained on WIC, and they received a child-care subsidy until he went to kindergarten. For his first three Christmases, her son was chosen for the Salvation Army angel tree, and he received gifts from a local donor. Delia was able to pay her most essential bills from her paycheck at work, but she and her son would not have been able to survive without the help they received from the state.

When her son was slightly older, Delia followed her director's earlier suggestion and applied for a scholarship to study early childhood education, and she was able to finish her associate's degree. Unfortunately, despite her years of steady employment and even with her degree, the director did not have the money in the budget to offer Delia a raise. At that point, Delia began to look for other options. She interviewed at several other child-care programs, and she was offered a job at a program that paid slightly more money and offered her the position of lead teacher. Delia had worked hard to get experience in her field and earn a degree. She had cared for hundreds of children and had helped their families while the parents were at work. Yet, she still needed the assistance of state support to raise her son.

After working that hard in her field, Delia should have been earning enough money to take care of her family on her own. The child-care system had let her down. Many child-care providers go through the same types of challenges as Delia. The system must be changed!

Chapter 3:
The Professional Perception

Although most child-care providers work for minimal wages, many early childhood specialists continue to work in the field because of their love for children. It is no secret that they may be paid just the minimum wage and have no health insurance, but for men and women who feel passionate about working with young children, early childhood programs are some of the best places to decide their career and make a difference in young lives. When dedicated educators work in an environment with support from their employers and from the parents of the children in their classrooms, they can still have a positive work experience. The quality of care that young children receive in child care can often be linked to the quality of working conditions that the child-care provider receives. When the child-care provider is treated poorly, it often leads to higher staff turnover that can have a negative effect on the children in the program.

Even though wages and benefits are at the heart of the issues regarding quality child care, respect and appreciation for child-care providers are also essential to maintaining consistent staffing in child-care programs. One sensitive issue for many child-care providers is the terminology that parents and community members often use to refer to the industry. The term *day care* has been used for decades to describe group child care for young children; however, this terminology is now frequently distinguished as a sign of disrespect by professionals who work with very young children. The source of the problem is where this term puts its emphasis: *day*. Although many child-care providers do care for young children during the day, supervision is only one part of an extensive job description. The term *child care* focuses on the child as the top priority. It also more comprehensively describes the many roles child-care providers actually undertake during the course of the day: supervisor, educator, nutritionist, chef, artist, planner, problem solver, mental-health specialist, nurse, special educator, and many other responsibilities.

RESPECT FOR THE ROLE OF CHILD-CARE PROVIDERS

With so many job responsibilities, it would be easy to surmise that child-care providers are esteemed members of the community. In some communities they are well respected, but often the individual faces are lumped into a broad category of blue-collar workers who are not acknowledged for their hard work. They may be looked down upon for their low-wage positions with hard-work demands. Many families may praise an individual child-care provider for his particular contribution to the family, but they often don't acknowledge the overall profession. Child-care providers often wish that families would simply understand the burden and sacrifices involved in their jobs and offer appreciation for those sacrifices.

Parents typically view their children as the most important thing in the world, as well they should. When they select a child-care program, they often focus on the individual teachers they are leaving their children with, instead of on the program as a whole. When a parent meets a teacher and finds that he has a loving and nurturing personality, the parent is more likely to leave the child in that teacher's care (Vanover, 2016). In fact, the teacher's personality is one of the top qualities considered by parents when selecting quality child care.

Respect for the Partnership

When parents work a full-time job, children are often in child care approximately nine to ten hours per day, including the parents' commute time. Most full-time working parents get to spend approximately two hours with their children each morning during the work week and two to three hours with them in the evening before bed. On weekends, they typically get to spend more time together, but many families have extracurricular obligations to fulfill when they are not at work. This means that on most days, a parent spends approximately five waking hours per day with the child, and the child-care provider may spend up to eight hours per day with the child. In a family child-care home, the same provider spends the entire day with the same children. Although the parents are always the experts on their children, the child-care provider becomes a significant part of the child's life, second only to the immediate family.

With that much influence and involvement in children's development, parents must acknowledge providers as key community members and even as an additional member of the family. Children who begin child care as infants will experience many of their first milestones while in child care. The child-care provider may see the child sit, crawl, and walk for the first time, before the family has the opportunity. Many children may even call the child-care provider *mama* or *dada* when first learning to speak. Child-care providers are thrilled to watch these special milestones in a child's life, but it is not their desire to steal these special moments from the family. The provider really wants to create an environment where he can communicate and share these moments with the family instead of making family members feel guilty for missing an important developmental moment. Once families realize that the provider and the parents are all on the same team to support the child, these relationships can work together to help the child be as successful as possible.

Respect for the Time

Child-care providers love the children they care for each day, and dedicated providers often think about the children when they are apart. The children are part of their lives; however, it is essential for parents to remember that the children the providers care for during the day are not their whole lives. Providers' own children and families are still most important to them. It is unrealistic for parents to assume that the child-care provider lives only in his job, and it is essential that they respect the educator's opportunity to be away from the job. Emailing, calling, and texting a child-care provider during his time away from work does not show respect for his individual lifestyle and family needs. This type of intrusive behavior crosses boundaries that would be unacceptable in many other industries. Families must remember to respect child-care providers' personal time.

It is also important for families to remember that, just as people do in every other profession, child-care providers have good days and bad days. The field of early education is a career that does not allow employees to come to work on autopilot. Child-care providers must give their time and attention to children as soon as they walk in the door to make sure that children do not get hurt. This constant level of supervision is always expected. At the same time, there will be days that the teachers are quiet and reserved due to reasons that are completely outside of the classroom environment. There will be days when a teacher may not be as affectionate as is his typical temperament. This is normal, and parents need to offer some grace in these situations. Caregivers are human beings. It is unrealistic to expect perfection.

Respect for the Learning Process

This same type of forgiveness must come into play when a child is experiencing challenging behaviors. For example, if the child goes through a phase of biting his classmates (as many toddlers do), the teacher will work with the family to prevent this situation as best as possible. The child-care program and the family can create a plan on how to reduce the behavior, but it is unrealistic for the family to expect the child-care provider to completely eliminate the behavior when he is caring for a classroom full of children. Likewise, if a child is learning to use the toilet, the teacher will make a plan to make sure he goes to the bathroom frequently throughout the day. However, if the child has a toileting accident, the family needs to be accepting that not all the child's behaviors are in the teacher's control, especially when he is taking care of multiple children.

Parents often focus on their own child's behavior and safety, which is their job. Child-care providers are focused on the safety of the entire group of children, so there may be small accidents when a child is in group child care. Occasional bumps and bruises will happen, because those are typical childhood injuries. Parents must understand that these are a natural part of growing up, not the fault of the child-care provider.

Respect for the Value

Finally, it is essential for families to understand that child-care providers are not being greedy when they ask for their payment. Tuition pays the child-care programs and minimal salaries for the staff. A pattern of late or missed payments can cause a program to be unable to stay open. It is that simple. Child-care providers understand that tuition payments can be challenging for families to make, so they are often willing to work out payment plans. At the same time, families must realize that if they are not paying for their slot, there is another family who will be willing to pay, and child-care providers must make the best decision in order to keep their businesses open.

When more families understand all these complicated aspects of the child-care providers' jobs, they are more likely to show respect and appreciation for all the hard work involved. Many child-care providers simply want to be told *thank you* for their work or for the family to acknowledge how important the provider is to the family. Some of the greatest gifts that early educators receive are cards and notes from families showing their appreciation. Child-care providers who feel appreciated are much more likely to stay in their teaching roles, and the children will benefit from that consistency in the long run.

COMPARING CHILD CARE WITH PUBLIC SCHOOL

Not all educators are treated equally. There is an enormous difference in the respect offered to teachers who work in the K-12 school system compared to early childhood educators who work with children ages birth to five. This does not mean that teachers in elementary schools and secondary schools receive the full amount of salary, support, or respect that they deserve. They too have challenging jobs, work long hours, and give up free time to support their students. They work with parents and families who might not support their efforts, and they often do not receive the appropriate amount of appreciation from their school boards, administrators, or the community. Despite the improvements that are still needed in the elementary and secondary education system, the early childhood education system does not receive even close to the same amount of respect that the teachers of older students receive.

Some of this discrepancy stems from changes to the early education system over time. When child care was first established, it was primarily focused on supervision and safety. This is much closer to what is typically considered babysitting. However, early education now looks much different. Not only are education and school readiness key components of early childhood education, but child-care providers also spend time conducting developmental assessments on each child in their care. They then use this information to develop a curriculum that is individually tailored to each student's goals, including children that are above or below the typical developmental milestones for their age range. Child-care providers design a classroom learning environment where children learn through play and interact with peers. While implementing high education standards in the classroom, teachers are also focused on health and safety standards and family communication. These job responsibilities are now on par with many of the responsibilities that are expected of kindergarten and primary teachers. Still, child-care providers are not treated the same.

One difference between elementary schools and child care is that child care is open when schools are not. Child care has always been a supplement for working parents who need a safe place for their children during summer break and school holidays. Child-care programs anticipate additional need during these breaks from elementary school and increase their staffing to prepare for the added children who will attend their programs. At the same time, child care also stays open when public school closes for unanticipated breaks, such as adverse weather or illness. Although some child-care programs may close for snow days, most attempt to stay open, both to support working families and to keep their weak budgets on target without losing necessary income.

Child care is a necessity, a fact that puts added pressure on child-care providers, directors, and owners. The COVID-19 pandemic highlighted this issue when states announced that the rate of infection was too high for staff and children in public schools to return to classrooms full time in the fall 2020 semester; however, child-care providers were expected to work during the same pandemic. Teachers across the United States had advocacy organizations speaking out on their behalf stating that going back to face-to-face classes potentially put their health at risk. No one fought the same battle for child-care providers. In fact, providers, families, and advocates all over the United States were fighting to open more capacity in child-care programs. Child-care providers were expected to take on responsibilities from which the public school system was exempt.

Public and private schools have benefited from a more consistent and unified voice and a more visible platform to publicize their needs and express their views. Because child-care programs in the United States include hundreds of thousands of small businesses, it is much more challenging to have a unified voice. Advocacy organizations such as NAEYC have attempted to speak for most child-care providers and to provide a strong statement on the importance of early childhood education and the need for professional treatment for child-care employees, but it is still hard to speak for so many independent organizations with such differing perspectives.

Elementary teachers are paid more for their work than child-care providers, and they also receive more support and resources for their classrooms. Some of the biggest differences include planning time and professional development. Most elementary teachers get some planning time each day that they can devote toward lesson plans, parent conferences, individualized education program (IEP) meetings, or parent communication. Many elementary teachers also have access to weekly or monthly team meetings with educators working with similar age groups, to help them align the school-wide curriculum. Even with these supports, many elementary teachers still work at home during off hours, but for child-care providers that may not be an option—it is simply a necessity.

Planning time at the individual and group level is extremely hard to find in child-care programs. Most child-care providers are required to post weekly lesson plans to allow parents an opportunity to review that week's classroom curriculum. However, providers often have to use their time at home, when they are not being paid, to do this planning. When they are working, they are with the children and required to meet adult-to-child ratios, so they cannot devote work time to writing lesson plans. Unlike many elementary-aged children, young children are not independent enough to keep themselves safe, so child-care providers cannot turn away from the children to focus on planning. Many teachers hope to do lesson planning during daily nap time; however, they must help children go to sleep and do necessary classroom cleaning first. Once cleaning is over, the first group of children often begin waking up from their naps, and the providers must begin interacting with those children to prevent them from waking up children who still need rest. This leaves little time for paperwork.

Professional-development time is just as challenging. All child-care providers, like elementary teachers, must continue learning and must attend professional-development training throughout the year. Most elementary teachers have designated days when the school is closed and teachers can attend training together. Some child-care programs attempt to close for a day or two during the year to offer staff training, but it can be a hardship for the families who need child care on those days. Consequently, most centers do not follow this practice. Many child-care programs encourage their teachers to attend trainings on the evenings or the weekends when they are not working with children. This can mean additional time away from their families and additional costs for training. Some child-care programs can pay the staff members for the hours they attended the training, but they may not be able to pay them for the cost of enrollment. Depending on where the child-care provider lives, access to high-quality training can be difficult, and the child-care provider may be expected to travel.

Finally, a significant difference between elementary school resources and child-care program resources is access to support for exceptional children. Elementary schools can usually work with school nurses, special educators, behavior analysts, mental-health specialists, occupational therapists, physical therapists, speech pathologists, and diagnosticians. These varied experts support the teachers by identifying children's special needs, assisting in individualizing learning, and helping to decrease negative behaviors. They also help to train the classroom teachers on how to approach such learning differences, so children with many different ability levels can thrive in the same classroom setting.

Children with special needs attend many different child-care programs, but these programs lack the supports available to schools. No specialist is available to train the child-care providers on how to help children with special needs succeed. Child-care providers are expected to be knowledgeable about many different diagnoses, and when they are not, they are deemed ill-equipped to work with these children. They are viewed as teachers who have not been trained properly to handle their jobs, even though teachers of older children often need the same coaching. Once a child-care provider feels defeated or inadequate to complete his job, it is hard to keep him motivated to stay in that position. Respect and support are essential for staffing consistency.

JAMIE'S CHOICE TO LEAVE

Unfortunately, a lack of respect and support can cause many talented child-care providers to leave the field permanently. Jamie initially starting working as a child-care provider after she received her master's degree in education. At first she applied for work in the public school system, but when limited jobs were available, she accepted a position at a very reputable early childhood center. Her focus for her master's degree had been elementary school, so an early childhood program was not significantly different. Her first position in the child-care program was working with infants. Jamie spent a lot of her time holding the babies, changing their diapers, feeding them, and rocking them to sleep. Although it wasn't the position she had planned on when getting her degree, she still felt that she was making a tremendous difference in the lives of young children.

The child-care program was high quality but could not offer Jamie a salary that was even comparable to the expected rate for someone with her educational achievement. At that point, even her boss did not have such a high level of education. Jamie worked in the field of early childhood education for a total of seven years, and her pay did slightly increase over time due to experience. When her own children were young, she also received a discount on the cost of their child care, but it was still not enough to compensate for her education.

Jamie's original reason for wanting to work in elementary education was because she wanted to help students establish a love of learning as soon as possible, so that they would be lifelong learners. Also, she had wanted to work with the youngest students possible, and the child-care center definitely gave her that opportunity. One of Jamie's favorite things about working with young children was that she loved getting to know each child and learning their personalities. Even though they were not her own children, she felt a strong connection to each of them, as if she were part of their families. Jamie also enjoyed her coworkers, who functioned as a team, with a plan for each day to take care of each of the children. Jamie and her team got to love them and watch them grow.

Although she had trained to be an elementary teacher, Jamie did not feel that her job as a child-care provider was any less important. She was still the teacher and caregiver of a classroom of students. She was still helping them learn new skills each day. She stayed in constant communication with the children's parents, and she made sure that each child felt safe and loved in her classroom. These were the same priorities that she had learned in her training programs.

After some time, there was an opening in the prekindergarten classroom, and Jamie transferred to work with slightly older students. This meant that Jamie began working on more curriculum and fewer basic needs. She was excited to prepare the children for kindergarten and watch them leave the program ready to move on to new challenges. After several years at the center, Jamie's boss, whom she enjoyed working for, transferred to another program. The new center had slightly higher salaries and more benefits for employees because it was attached to a larger company. When a position at the other center opened, Jamie and several of her coworkers transferred.

The new program initially seemed to support the teachers much more than had Jamie's previous center. The increase in salary and availability of health insurance were better than before, and the company's administrative support for the child-care program was also an improvement, offering more materials for the classrooms and a much larger playground space. However, over time, Jamie began to see a difference in the families she worked with at the new program. There were some families at the program who seemed to have unrealistic expectations of what the program should be teaching their children or what Jamie's job responsibilities were.

At one point in her career, Jamie had felt very much respected as an early childhood educator, but that slowly began to change. Jamie felt more discouraged than before. Several times, she sat down with a family to discuss concerns about a child's learning needs and found that her opinion was not valued. Even though kindergarten was quickly approaching for these children, the families ignored Jamie's concerns, which would eventually lead to a negative impact for their children. Jamie also began to be upset every time she was told that she worked in a "daycare" instead of a school, or when someone would say that she was a babysitter. She began to question herself when she did not receive respect from the children in her classroom and from their families.

During her last year working as a child-care provider, Jamie had a classroom of students with very demanding parents. In the past, parents had focused more on whether their children were ready for kindergarten before leaving her classroom. This group of parents seemed to look for details to argue about. Jamie also noticed that parents wanted to specifically blame her for challenging behaviors that some of the students demonstrated at school. When she tried to collaborate with the families to work through the problems, they were more interested in assigning fault for the situation than in helping the children resolve the behaviors. It was difficult to get the support she needed because her boss, whom Jamie respected and trusted, was dealing with a major health issue at the time and was less available. One of Jamie's biggest concerns was that she was not being the best teacher that she could be because she was constantly being criticized by the classroom parents. Her attention was focused on defending herself instead of working with her students.

For years Jamie's position as a child-care provider had worked well for her family. Her children had been at the program with her when they were younger, and the tuition discount had helped with finances. She had never had to work nights and weekends, so she could have time with her husband and children. Now that Jamie's children were in elementary school, the job seemed less flexible. If one of her children was sick, it was harder for her to stay home, because she was still needed to support the classroom ratio. Now she was bringing home the stress of working with a classroom of difficult parents for a low-wage job. It seemed that a position in child care was no longer benefitting Jamie's family, and she needed to make a change.

Jamie accepted a new position in purchasing at a state organization. Her pay was higher than the child-care program, and her job offered flexibility if she needed to take time off for one of her daughters. She also had the opportunity to work from home if needed, and the company had lots of opportunities for promotion, which rarely happens in child care. Jamie's new position allowed her to work on specific projects that had distinct timelines and offered her the freedom to problem solve as long as she met her deadlines. When she made recommendations to her section and her boss, she was respected for her expert opinion.

Jamie had found it very difficult to leave child care. She had worked with hundreds of children in the seven years that she spent in the field. She remembered every child, because each one had taught her something while she had the opportunity to work with them. She had loved watching them grow and learn. One of Jamie's favorite moments with each of her students was that moment when she could see the light in their eyes because they finally understood a new skill. She was going to miss that moment, but she could still watch her own children learn and grow.

Unfortunately, Jamie's story is not unique. Many child-care providers are not considered experts in their field, even though they work with children each day. Administrators and families forget to show their appreciation, and early childhood teachers become discouraged. When a teacher is overwhelmed with feelings of inadequacy or self-doubt, it is hard to be the best teacher possible. It is essential for the child-care field and communities to show early educators the respect they need to help our young children be as successful as possible.

Chapter 4:
Streams of Funding

The child-care system receives funding from many different financial streams, yet the system is grossly underfunded throughout the United States. The funding streams include money from the federal government, state governments, grants and donations, and parents. These streams come together to support a system that is still drastically in need of financial support; however, to understand how the system is broken, it is important to understand how the current streams come together in an attempt to prop up a dilapidated system.

Many of the funding sources support only one specific purpose, so it can be complicated to attempt to braid the funding together to assist the field as a whole. For example, if one source of funding is used specifically for low-income families, those funds cannot be used to support the vast majority of families who must pay out of pocket for their child-care expenses. The best way to determine how to use the funding streams most effectively is to learn about their intended uses in order to pair them with similar funding.

FEDERAL FUNDING

One of the largest sources of funding for the child-care system comes from the federal government. The Child Care and Development Block Grant (CCDBG), section 418 of the Social Security Act, 42 U.S.C. 618, provides funding throughout the United States and its territories to support quality, monitor health and safety, and assist with child-care subsidies for low-income families. This block grant went into effect in 1992 (Office of Child Care [OCC], 2020); the most recent revisions occurred in 2016. The federal government issues the block grant funding to the states and territories, and they distribute the funds throughout their jurisdiction to support families.

CCDBG Priorities

The top priority of the grant is to support low-income families so that their children can enroll in child care while the adults are working or attending school (OCC, 2020). The grant also focuses on maintaining health and safety throughout all regulated child-care programs, including supporting background checks of employees working in these facilities. Even though the grant focuses on families at financial risk, the health and safety measures benefit all children enrolled in child-care programs. The federal funds issued to benefit low-income families allow parents to work or to go to school without having to worry about whether their children are in a safe and quality child-care environment (OCC, 2020).

The block grant funds also emphasize that each grantee must provide consumer education for parents and the community about what quality child care looks like. The idea behind this requirement is that, with consumer education in place, parents are more likely to select higher-quality child-care programs, and the demand for quality child-care programs will increase, causing programs to improve to compete with the market.

CCDBG Requirements

The requirements of a block grant can be extremely confusing. In general, a block grant is a lump sum from the federal government that must be used in support of a broad range of programs. Many agencies interpret a block grant to allow flexible spending, as long as the general purpose of the grant falls within the intended area of aid.

The CCDBG, on the other hand, has some very specific requirements for the funding issued throughout the country. First, 70 percent of the funding must be spent on direct services (OCC, 2020). The most important purpose of the money is to help children and families, so it must find its way to the programs that benefit those families. This instantly limits the amount of money that can be used for administration and system infrastructure. Five percent or less of the grant may be spent on administration (OCC, 2020).

The grant also requires that funding be spent toward improving the quality of child-care programs. It specifies that a total of 12 percent of the funds be spent on initiatives to improve quality. Out of that 12 percent, a total of 3 percent is supposed to be spent on infant and toddler initiatives to support the youngest and most vulnerable in the child-care population (OCC, 2020).

Some funding must be spent on health and safety measures, background checks, consumer education for parents, and training for child-care providers. A portion of the health and safety dollars typically goes toward a monitoring system for the regulated child-care programs throughout the state (OCC, 2020). This program may be administered through the state's Office of the Inspector General or a similar organization that focuses on inspecting institutions to ensure that they meet the minimum requirements for regulated facilities. The professional-development and training requirements include a professional-development system that allows child-care providers to progress through a professional-development ladder that can help them attain higher levels of certification and more knowledge in the field (OCC, 2020).

The revisions to the grant in 2016 encourage all states and territories to increase their funding over time so that subsidy funding for low-income families can cover the cost of 75 percent of the regulated child-care programs throughout the state (OCC, 2020). This subsidy is offered primarily to families who fall within the state's or territory's income guidelines, are working or are in an education program, and have children younger than thirteen years of age. There is also an exception for children with physical or mental disabilities. For example, a family with a child up to nineteen years old who is incapable of being left alone to care for herself may receive subsidy funds to use for care of that child, as long as the family doesn't earn more than 85 percent of the state's median income (OCC, 2020).

Each state or territory will reimburse child care at a slightly different rate, because the cost of living in the state and the market rate for child care vary from area to area. If a state reimburses at 50 percent of the market rate of child care, then the subsidy amount would cover the full cost of child care at half the centers in the state (OCC, 2020). Families who receive the subsidy can still attend the other, more expensive centers in the state, but the family would be responsible for paying the overage cost at those centers beyond what the subsidy would cover.

The block grant requires that families who qualify for the subsidy have some choice as to where to send their children and not be assigned by the state or territory to the next available slot. To offer that choice, the family must be issued a subsidy certificate or voucher to take to the center of their choice (OCC, 2020). The block grant allows center-based child-care programs and family child-care homes to receive subsidy funding from eligible families as long as they are licensed, regulated, or registered according to the state's requirements (OCC, 2020). This typically includes meeting mandatory background checks and health and safety measures.

To receive this funding from the federal government, the states and territories also have obligations to fulfill. First, the states and territories must provide a financial match of their own to partner with the federal funds that are devoted to child care. This requirement was established in the Child Care and Development Funding (CCDF) State Match Provisions Final Rule (OCC, 2012). The amount of the match that each grantee provides is determined by the current Federal Medical Assistance Percentage rate in that state at the time of the financial award.

The state is also obligated to write a plan that will show how the funds will be distributed over a three-year period and how the state will meet the requirements listed in the CCDF Final Rule that is current at the time of the plan. The plan must include the reimbursement rate for the subsidy program. That rate is set in accordance with the data received every three years when the state conducts a market-rate survey for the cost of child care (OCC, 2020). Once the market rate of care is established, the state can set the percent of reimbursement that is possible based on the CCDBG funds, any additional state funds, and the cost of care throughout the state.

The three-year plan must also include how the state or territory will support special at-risk populations. Along with serving children of families who receive low wages, the state must also identify how to support children who experience homelessness, are living in foster care, have special needs, and/or are English language learners (OCC, 2020). Most child care focuses on preschool, but the three-year plan must also identify ways to support infant and toddler child care and school-age child care. By creating a plan that serves each of these groups, the states and territories can ensure opportunities to thrive and succeed are available to the widest possible range of families and children.

The CCDBG also issues funds that support Head Start and Early Head Start programs throughout the country. These grants are not administered by the states themselves; instead, individual organizations in a state can apply to receive these funds directly from the federal government. To qualify for Head Start or Early Head Start programs, families must be living at or below the federal poverty level. The federal government issues approximately $9 billion annually to support Head Start programs throughout the United States.

Other Federal Funding

A smaller source of child-care funding from the federal government is the Temporary Assistance for Needy Families (TANF), which was established in 1996. TANF funding is intended for the following four purposes:

- Provide funding to help families care for their children in their own homes

- Provide funding for job preparation, work, and marriage

- Provide funding to reduce unwanted pregnancies

- Provide funding to support two-parent families

Although TANF funds are primarily used for housing and other supports for families, the law does allow up to 30 percent of TANF funds to be transferred to assist with a state's child-care subsidy (US Department of Health and Human Services, 2012). Most states with a large population of families in need cannot spare 30 percent of their TANF funding for child care, but many states may be able to offer some of these funds toward child care to supplement their CCDBG funds.

Some sporadic sources of child-care funding through federal grant opportunities are also available: the two most recent opportunities for early childhood education grants include the Race to the Top Grant and the Preschool Development Grant. During the application period for each of these grants, each state and territory had the opportunity to apply for funding. The federal grant application process can be extensive, and state organizations such as the department of education and child and family services must collaborate to receive the maximum number of incentives possible. The Race to the Top grant offered one billion dollars to child-care programs in twenty states and the District of Columbia (US Department of Health and Human Services, 2013). The Preschool Development Grant, currently in round two, has offered $275 million to early education programs in fiscal year 2020 (First Five Years Fund, 2019).

STATE FUNDING

State funding for child-care programs varies widely depending on the state in question. All states receiving federal CCDBG funding must provide the mandatory matching dollars that are reserved for critical child-care funding. But, beyond the CCDBG match, states are not required to budget any additional dollars for child care. Some states, such as Connecticut, invest a large amount of state dollars into additional child-care initiatives that could not be covered by CCDBG dollars alone.

Others, such as Kentucky, can meet only the mandatory match to CCDBG funds but cannot offer any other funding. Their state budget dollars are desperately needed in areas other than child care.

In all states, the funding that typically goes to early childhood education supports state-funded public preschool for three- and four-year-old children. These programs are most often focused on children from families who are financially at risk or on children who have a developmental delay that requires them to have an IEP with support services before starting kindergarten.

Based on an individual state's funding, public preschool can look very different. Florida, for example, currently offers universal pre-K that serves both low-income and middle-income families with four-year-old students (Office of Early Learning, n.d.). Some states offer full-day public preschool (approximately a seven-hour school day), and others offer a half-day program. However, if children are in public preschool for only three to four hours per day, working families will still need child care for a large portion of the day. This means that many families throughout the United States must use both public school and child care to care for their children and complete a full work day.

Some public preschool programs may partner with a federally funded Head Start program or a licensed child-care program to extend the time available for care for young children. For example, if a public school program and a Head Start program partner in caring for children who qualify for both programs, they could receive double the amount of funding for the children and care for them for an extended amount of time each day. This option also allows the children and families to receive more support services. Child-care programs may also partner with state-funded preschool programs in the same manner.

OTHER FUNDING SOURCES

The predominant source of funding for child care in the United States is families. Families spend $42 billion on child care annually (Gould and Blair, 2020). Based on the cost of child care throughout the United States, data show that child care is the largest monthly expense for most families with young children (Child Care Aware of America, 2019). Child-care costs are even surpassing families' housing costs in the majority of states. Recognizing the burden that these costs place on families who utilize child-care programs, centers and family child-care homes are limited in what they can charge and, therefore, equally constrained as to what they can pay their child-care providers. This creates an unending cycle in which child-care programs charge what they can (instead of what they are worth) and pay the providers a limited salary. Providers then leave the field to find higher-paying jobs. In the end, the children are the most affected by the repeated loss of adult caregivers to whom they have grown attached.

Some child-care programs may try to offset the cost of care for families through fundraising. These fundraisers range from selling chocolate bars to having annual yard sales to hosting golf scrambles. Despite the fact that the programs are brainstorming to find ways to reduce tuition, many fundraising costs come back to the families themselves. Parents and grandparents are usually the individuals who purchase the chocolate bars or pay to participate in the golf scrambles. Not only do they invest their own money in the fundraising programs, but families often invest hours of their time to help lead these initiatives. If a child-care program can choose a fundraiser that attracts the majority of its participation from the broader community rather than the enrolled families, then the proceeds from the event can actually offset the cost of care. Unfortunately, these types of fundraising events can be challenging to plan and execute.

Larger-scale donations are a method of receiving funding without causing additional stress to the enrolled families. Child-care programs may solicit donations from community businesses or employers of the families enrolled in the child-care programs. The businesses benefit by receiving a tax write-off for their donations and by the opportunity to advertise to the families enrolled in the child-care programs themselves. Companies may find it beneficial to donate to a child-care program that their employees use, not only as a tax deduction, but also as a way to subsidize the cost of the employees' child care and minimize staff turnover.

Another method of funding for child-care programs must be acknowledged. The cost of child-care tuition throughout the United States is subsidized by the extremely low wages that are paid to professional child-care providers. These education professionals are carrying the cost of care on their own backs. If child-care providers were paid a living wage, child care would indeed be more expensive—perhaps too expensive for most middle-income families to afford. As the situation stands, although tuition remains quite high, child-care rates are somewhat lowered because our child-care providers are denied the salaries and benefits that they need to care for their own families. Even with a combination of tuition, fundraisers, state funding, and federal funding, the industry cannot find a way to pay child-care employees a fair wage. There is simply not enough funding coming into the system to support the needed outcomes. Funding from established sources must be increased, and new funding sources must be incorporated into the equation so that consistent child care can be offered to all children who need it and child-care providers can earn the income that they need to pay their bills and stay in a stable career.

A STATE-LEVEL VIEW

Stephanie works for her state's department for health and family services, and it is her job to oversee the funding sent to her state through the CCDBG. Along with supervising those funds, Stephanie helps to oversee all of the child-care programs in her state, including centers and family child-care homes. Her state is one of the most expensive in the United States for child-care costs, and there is not a sufficient amount of child care available based on the number of working families who need it. Almost 750,000 children in her state need child care.

CCDBG funding is not the only source of funding available to child care in Stephanie's state. Over the past five to ten years, her state has tried to increase the amount of state funding in an attempt to make it more closely match the funds offered by the federal government. The ratio has been anywhere from 70 percent federal and 30 percent state to 60 percent federal and 40 percent state. Although the state could be a little more flexible in the application of its funding, its leaders have decided that the state funds should be used in accordance with the CCDBG funds and follow the same policies.

The 8,200 regulated child-care programs in Stephanie's state provide 250,000 slots for young children. The subsidy program funds approximately 55,000 of those children at one time. That means that only about 20 percent of the slots throughout the state are funded by the child-care subsidy. Those children receive a voucher that can be presented to a child-care program at the time of enrollment, allowing the child-care program to bill the state for the cost of the child's care.

Eighty percent of the slots offered in the state come from parents providing the out-of-pocket expenses. Because only 20 percent of the total available slots are served through the subsidy program, approximately 13,000 children are on the waiting list to receive state subsidy funds. Of the 8,200 programs in the state, half accept a subsidy; those 4,000-plus programs can be divided into three categories regarding how much of their income is reliant on subsidy:

- Approximately one-third of the child-care programs in the state rely predominantly on subsidy funds.

- Another third of the child-care programs receive approximately half of their funding from a subsidy.

- The final third of the child-care programs receive almost no funding from families who utilize a child-care subsidy.

If a child-care program does not accept subsidy funds at all, then the program's entire income must be funded by the families it serves.

The voucher system is also set up to assist high-need populations such as children with special needs or families living in homelessness, as well as to reserve spots for infants and toddlers instead of focusing solely on the preschool population. Stephanie's state dedicates a certain number of vouchers to these at-risk populations to make sure that they are not underrepresented in the child-care system. Unfortunately, like many other states, Stephanie's state lacks enough vouchers to meet the needs of at-risk populations.

When Stephanie looks at child-care access throughout her state, she can see areas where child care is significantly lacking. No community in the state has enough regulated child care to meet the needs of the community. Because almost 750,000 children in her state need child care and only about 250,000 spots are available in regulated child-care programs, supply and demand keeps driving up the cost of care. Many families cannot afford these high costs. Most areas have enough child care for approximately one-third of the families who need it; the rural areas have even less. Some smaller communities may be able to meet the needs in their area, but overall there is a huge lack of care. Some unregulated family child-care homes operate in the state, but one of the largest sources of child care is families who use nannies or au pairs. It can be less expensive to hire an au pair, particularly when a family has several children, than it will be to pay for multiple children to attend a regulated child-care program.

This does not mean that it is inexpensive to hire a nanny or an au pair. There was actually legislative action in Stephanie's state several years ago to ensure fair working conditions for nannies and au pairs so that they do not work long hours without appropriate compensation. Families have to find someone to watch their children, so they attempt to make the best decision they can for their circumstances.

When Stephanie looks at her state's child-care system as a whole, she sees significant flaws that need to be addressed. Stephanie is worried that the state's voucher process undermines the stability of the child-care system. When a child who uses a voucher needs to move locations, the state stops paying for that slot at the original center. That center experiences a gap in funding until a child can be found to fill the slot. Yet, the educators must still be paid. Fixed expenses such as the mortgage, utilities, and insurance premiums must be paid. The cost of that slot in the classroom does not diminish, but the funding from the state is not consistent. Instead of using a voucher payment system, Stephanie would rather the state switch to a classroom funding method. Federal and state funding could be used to keep a classroom open consistently, even when a child transitions from one classroom to another, or from one center to a different one.

The state model for child care currently operates on a per-child basis; a per-customer system is not used for any other industry. For example, if the state funds the transportation system or public broadcasting system, it provides an annual budget. That budget is divided over twelve months to create an average funding amount that can be expected by the individual units. This allows each company to set a regular budget based on known income and expenditures. Stephanie believes that, for child care in her state to be successful and stable, the annual-budget system must apply.

This money—with fewer income fluctuations—would allow child-care programs to establish a higher level of quality without unplanned tuition increases for families. If the child-care system followed the same model as the public school system and set a one-year budget based on the number of students served the previous year, that would provide consistent funding. The child-care system could then provide consistent quality related to the planned expenses for the number of children estimated in the upcoming fiscal year.

Stephanie is also concerned about the early childhood workforce in her state. Workforce supports for child-care employees are desperately needed, because child-care providers need to be able to pay their employees a livable wage. Child-care programs receive funding through subsidies and other measures, but those funds are not going into the paychecks of the child-care providers. Her state's current child-care budget is set up so that the programs have a wide variety of coaching and resources available to providers. These offerings are great for helping providers to do their jobs well and learn more about the field, yet the money invested in these resources does not help child-care providers to feed their families.

Many child care programs do not have the funding to offer their employees salary increases based on education and experience. If the child-care programs want to attract higher-quality employees, they will have to compensate them financially.

Stephanie believes that her state has pushed the current subsidy system as far as it can possibly go. The industry needs a completely new financial structure that demands and supports higher wages for caregivers as well as high-quality care—two aspects that are inextricably linked.

Right now, the state can only shut down a child-care program for health and safety causes, so a lack of quality that does not directly affect the children's overall health and safety is not penalized. The public school system is not monitored by the same scale. The public school infrastructure monitors quality, with health and safety only being one small piece of that equation.

If the child-care infrastructure were changed to look more like the public school system, parents would not only expect quality, but they could also demand improvements where quality was lacking. Child-care programs would be held accountable for quality, and in turn, they would hire professionals who can demonstrate quality, driving the pay rate up to a livable wage. This does not mean that child-care programs would have to be state institutions. Plenty of elementary and secondary schools are privately run and still held to the same standards of accountability as the public school system; some may push that level of quality much higher than the public school requirements. The idea is not to change ownership of the child-care programs from the small-business owner but to change the public expectation enough so that parents expect quality and will not settle for less.

Stephanie's vision for her state's child-care system includes some dramatic changes; however, it also addresses some of the key issues that many states are struggling with. These goals need to be delivered in all states, not just in Stephanie's area of the country. Paying for reimbursement on a per-child basis creates instability for all child-care programs; child-care providers need consistent funding to support annual budgets. The amount of federal subsidy offered to the individual states does not cover the number of families who need support for child care; funding must increase to meet the need. Child-care access is stretched all over the United States, and when families can't find affordable regulated child care, they look for alternatives. Higher-quality programs that pay high-quality employees a livable wage are necessary.

In the next chapter, we examine more closely the burden our current system places on families.

Chapter 5:
The Burden on the Family

Child care is essential for the working family, but child care can also be a constant source of stress. For the adults in the home to go to work, they must find child care that is safe, affordable, and of high quality. It must be close enough to the home that the adults can drop the child off in time to get to work, and it must be open during the hours that the adults are working, no matter what time of day that is. Most importantly, there must be an available slot for the child so that the parents can obtain the child care they need. All these potential barriers—cost, location, hours of operation, quality, and availability—can have a significant impact on whether or not a parent can continue to work after a child is born.

High-quality child care has many benefits for young children besides providing a safe location for the child to be while the adults are at work. Children have the opportunity to be in a social environment with other children to learn how to play together, take turns, and follow directions. Early childhood classrooms provide learning environments where children can explore and experiment with hands-on activities. Children can benefit when skilled early childhood educators conduct developmental assessments to make sure that each child is developing with no signs of delays. If developmental delays are suspected, the teachers can help the families obtain support from pediatricians and other specialists. It is essential for parents to find the programs that best support their families.

THE LARGEST FAMILY EXPENSE

The greatest barrier to high-quality child care is cost. High-quality programs typically hire better-educated teachers, pay them higher salaries, and reduce the adult-to-child ratio, so that children can spend more individualized time with their teachers. These factors make it harder for child-care programs to stay financially stable; therefore, they have to charge more for tuition.

Research done by the Center for American Progress shows that families making the state median income spend approximately 18 percent of their income on infant care or 13 percent of their income on toddler care (Workman and Jessen-Howard, 2018). This is well above the Child Care for Working Families Act budgetary guideline of 7 percent of the family income being spent on child care. (Author note: At the time of this writing, the bill is in committee in the US Senate.) In fact, there is no state in the United States where the cost of infant care is below the recommended 7 percent of the state median income (Workman and Jessen-Howard, 2018). Again, this data is based on the family having one child in child care at a time, so families with several children in child care can spend a much larger portion of their income.

Regardless of the state, parents carry the largest financial burden of the child-care system: approximately $42 billion per year (Gould and Blair, 2020). These huge costs have caused many families to delay having children, plan on having fewer children, or space the births farther apart so that their children are not in care at the same time. Infant care is now often more expensive than a year of college tuition or monthly mortgage payments.

The annual report issued by Child Care Aware (CCA) of America (2019) shows cost comparisons throughout the United States by dividing the country into four regions: Midwest, Northeast, South, and West. In the Midwest, for example, the average cost of center-based, full-time child care for two children in 2018 was $20,914; the average cost of college tuition for one student was $10,083; and the average cost of housing was $17,797. The Northeast and South regions have similar costs. The West region is the only one in the United States where full-time, center-based child care is not the most expensive budget item for a family with two children; there, housing ($23,271) is only slightly more expensive than child care ($21,327). In the Midwest, Northeast, and South regions, child care is more expensive than housing and every other typical monthly expense for families (CCA, 2019).

Some families see these high costs as a temporary situation and an investment in their careers and their families' futures. Lindsay Powers (2020) wrote in *The New York Times* that if she left her job while her children were young just to avoid astronomical child-care costs, she would not be able to re-enter the workforce at the same level position as when she left. The investment in her career, along with the reassurance of knowing that her children are in quality child care, gives her the comfort to continue paying extremely high child-care fees. Her family is exceptional, however: they are able to offset the cost of child care by simply reducing their spending and not eating out as frequently. Both she and her husband have high-paying positions, so they can choose to make sacrifices for a few years while their children need expensive care.

The 2019 CCA of America report (2019) showed that 24 percent of American families were led by single mothers in 2018, and the average median income for a family headed by a single mother is $26,141. This means that the option of paying for expensive child care for only a few years is simply not available. It isn't about making a sacrifice. The focus is on making sure that the basic needs of the family are met, and the cost of child care can be a significant burden.

COMPARING THE ALTERNATIVES

Regulated child care includes center-based child care and family child-care homes. Both types of child care must follow state regulations, such as background checks for staff members, adherence to health and safety standards, and implementation of a developmentally appropriate curriculum. Regulated child care must undergo inspections by a state agency to make sure that it is meeting the demands of the state requirements. This type of care may participate in the government child-care subsidy program, so it can be very beneficial for low-wage families who need help paying for child care. When regulated child care is not available, families may have to look at alternatives to make sure that their children are not left unsupervised.

When families do not have access to, or choose not to use, regulated child care, many look for other options. This can include hiring an au pair or hourly sitter, joining with friends in a nanny-share arrangement, participating in co-op care, or choosing family-member care. Every option has advantages and disadvantages, so it is important for families to consider every possible scenario.

Many families may prefer individualized care for their children and choose to hire a nanny or au pair. This allows the family to set the hours and job requirements that are needed for their particular circumstances. Without the state regulations and inspections of licensed child care, the family must complete background checks on the nanny, explain healthy habits that are required in the home, monitor the curriculum the nanny is using, and make sure that the children still have opportunities to socialize with other children. Hiring a nanny or au pair is a high-cost option, so many families will not have the opportunity to use this type of care.

A nanny share can give families the opportunity for the children to be in a very small group, build necessary social skills, and still receive individualized attention. Sharing can be less expensive than the cost of one family having an individual au pair or nanny, since the cost of care is split among the participating families. The families participating in the nanny share would have to agree upon the candidate to watch the children and jointly determine the pay rate, location of care, and what type of curriculum or activities the children will engage in during the day. It may be challenging for a nanny to provide appropriate activities for children of different age groups. Parents also need to consider the education and experience of the nanny, as well as the background-check process. Families would also need to see whether there are state laws that prohibit a nanny or child-care provider from caring for more than three children at one time without going through the regulation process.

A parent co-op is similar to a nanny share, but instead of paying a nanny to watch the children, the parents take turns watching each other's children. A parent co-op may not cost the family any money, but the parent would need to have a flexible schedule to be able to care for the children one day a week or one week per month. Also, all the parents in the co-op would need to feel comfortable caring for a group of children at one time. Even if the parents in the co-op are acquainted with one another, it is important that they all sit down in advance to discuss their ideas on curriculum, nutrition, and discipline so that there are not disagreements between the families. Background checks may still be desired if the parents do not know one another well.

Parents of young children may prefer to have a family member watch their children, but this option depends a great deal on whether or not there are family members in the area who are available. It can be very comforting for parents to have a grandparent or another family member watch their children during the day, especially since a family member will typically honor the cultural beliefs of the family when caring for the children. Parents need to remember that if they choose this option, they are essentially entering a business relationship with the family member, whether or not they pay for child care. It may be more uncomfortable to require a family member to discipline in a certain way, serve particular foods, or use a specific curriculum when caring for the child. If the parents are looking for a very structured environment, they will need to speak with the family member in advance to see if the caregiver is willing to follow their wishes.

LOW-WAGE FAMILIES

A low-wage family is typically defined as a family whose income is at or less than 200 percent of the FPL (Rachidi, 2019). Many families who fall into the low-wage category do not pay for child care outside the home. They typically rely on care provided by a parent or grandparent. A parent caring for her own child in the home may place her family in the low-wage category, because she is giving up her opportunity to provide income for the family. Some families are purposefully making this sacrifice because it is important to them for one of the parents to stay at home until the child is old enough to start kindergarten. Other families would prefer the opportunity for the adults in the home to be able to work outside of the home and contribute to the income, but the cost of child care is too expensive for this to happen.

As noted earlier in this book, each state and territory in the United States has a child-care subsidy system for low-wage families so the adults in the household can work. Unfortunately, there may not be enough funding available to provide the support these families need. In 2017, the National Women's Law Center documented that twenty different states had waiting lists for their child-care subsidy programs. The same study also found that five of those states (Florida, Massachusetts, Mississippi, North Carolina, and Texas) had more than 20,000 children on the subsidy waiting list in their state. Because of the backlogs, many of those families would no longer need access to child care by the time their names were taken off the waiting list. The same study by the National Women's Law Center (2017) also showed that many of the families who did qualify for subsidies still had to pay more than 7 percent of the family's total income to allow their children to attend child care, even with government funds.

Higher-income families are twice as likely as low-wage families to use regulated child care, simply due to the associated cost (Malik, 2019). Low-wage families may find that they have to consider other options: relative care or self-care. Relative care can be the nuclear family, grandparents, or another relative. Self-care is when the child has some amount of time alone in a home and must care for himself or herself, including preparing meals and maintaining hygiene routines. Unlike regulated care, which must meet minimum state standards in order to operate, relative care and self-care (obviously) do not adhere to state requirements.

Working families are families in which all the adults in the home must work outside of the home, so that the children need more formalized child care. Thirty percent of working families are considered low-wage families (Malik, 2019). Of this 30 percent, only four out of ten families pay for child care, meaning that they use relative care or self-care for their children. Of the four out of ten families who use regulated care, 35 percent of their family budget is used for their child-care needs (Malik, 2019).

It is also important to consider that formalized child care is typically offered Monday through Friday during daytime hours. Many low-wage jobs require their employees to work nights and weekends, as well as daytime hours. Regulated child care typically has set business hours that may only be altered during an emergency related to weather or utility issues with the building; however, relative care or other unregulated child care may not be as reliable, so the family must make many different arrangements to ensure that the child has care when needed.

Due to alternative schedules, half the children who need child care must have more than one arrangement to cover the family's hours of work (Malik, 2019). In fact, one-fourth of children in child care need *three or more* arrangements to cover the necessary hours of care (Malik, 2019). For many low-wage families, more arrangements may be needed if some sources of child care are not reliable.

THE IMPACT ON MOTHERS

Even in a family where all the adults in the home work outside of the home, the responsibility for making child-care arrangements typically falls to the mother. In fact, a survey conducted by the Center for American Progress in 2018 showed that mothers are 40 percent more likely than fathers to report a negative impact to their careers due to child care (Schochet, 2019). This means that many mothers have to work fewer hours, take a pay reduction, or leave their jobs when child-care arrangements do not work out for the family. Research from CCA of America (2019) indicates that 39 percent of working mothers are solely responsible for staying at home with a child when the child is too sick to attend child care or elementary school. CCA of America (2019) also indicates that only 53 percent of mothers of elementary school students are employed full time outside of the home, largely due to the average 29 days off during the school year, not counting summer vacation. Mothers are typically called upon to fill in those gaps when elementary schools are closed.

That does not mean that all mothers want to be the adult in the home who sacrifices career opportunities to stay home with the children when they do not have alternative child care. The 2018 study by the Center for American Progress states that the majority of mothers would take more steps to advance their careers and increase their income if they knew they had reliable, affordable child care (Schochet, 2019).

The COVID-19 pandemic has specifically highlighted the differences in child-care responsibilities between mothers and fathers. When child care became hard to find due to mandated closures and restrictions, mothers began to work from home and care for their children at the same time. Many mothers have stated that they began waking early and going to bed later to complete their job responsibilities, so they could care for their children during the day (Goldberg, 2020). In cases where the employer would not let employees adjust their work hours or work from home, more women than men had to leave their jobs or significantly reduce their work hours (Goldberg, 2020). With prolonged reductions in child care during this type of health emergency, the United States could see a potential reduction of women in the workforce that will be felt for years to come.

SEARCHING FOR QUALITY CARE

When Maria found out that she was pregnant with her first child, she immediately began to make plans for child care. Several of her close friends had had children before her, and all of them said that finding a child-care spot for an infant was very challenging. She began calling centers to set up tours before she and her husband had even told many of their friends that they were expecting.

At her first baby shower, Maria had a conversation with a family member who offered to watch the baby for the first year or two so Maria and her husband would not have to place him in a child-care center. Her cousin stayed at home each day caring for her own toddler, so this seemed like a mutually beneficial situation. Maria would feel very comfortable leaving her son with a member of her family, and instead of paying the high fees of a child-care program, she could pay a reasonable rate to a family member who would appreciate the extra income. Plus, the children would enjoy playing together as they grew up. Maria and her husband agreed to the arrangement, and they stopped looking for outside child care.

Once her son was born, Maria took the eight weeks of maternity leave offered by her employer. Due to some mild complications, including a low-grade fever after her Cesarean section, Maria and the baby stayed in the hospital for a full week. Once they were home and feeling better, friends and family came to visit and meet the baby for the first time. One of the first visitors was her cousin who was going to watch her son when Maria went back to work. The visit seemed very awkward at first, but Maria assumed that it must have been because she hadn't slept in a week. After about twenty minutes, her cousin announced that she was expecting another baby. Maria was thrilled for her family, but she was also apprehensive about where the conversation was headed. Her cousin explained that, since she had had complications with her last pregnancy, the doctor was immediately categorizing this pregnancy as high risk and was going to be watching her very closely. She would be limited on physical activity and how much she could lift. She would not be able to watch Maria's son as they had planned.

Without saying a word, Maria instantly began to panic. She was already a week and a half into her maternity leave. She only had six and a half weeks left to find a quality child-care program where she felt comfortable leaving her son while she was at work each day. This change would also mean an increase in the amount of money that Maria and her husband had budgeted for the baby's care, since all the child-care centers seemed to be more expensive than home-based child care. Maria was grateful when the baby began to cry and she could tell her guests that it was time for her son to eat. They decided to leave, and as Maria fed her newborn, she opened her laptop to search all the child-care programs in her area that provided infant care.

For three days, when she wasn't busy feeding or changing her son, she called programs in her area to check their cost and availability. Most programs that she called had a significant waiting list. The center directors told her that they give priority to siblings of children who are already enrolled. When she asked for the approximate length of the waiting list, many directors told her between eight months and a year. Maria would have to quit her job if she could not find child care before that time, but the family budget depended on two incomes, so both Maria and her husband needed to work to afford quality health insurance and pay all their bills. She carried the family health insurance as one of her job benefits, and insurance was essential given all the doctor visits that a newborn baby would require. A couple of programs put Maria's name on the waiting list just in case there was an opening, but she knew that the possibility was very low.

Maria was able to find five programs that could have an opening for an infant in the next few months, so as soon as the doctor approved her to drive again, she set up tours. The first program she saw seemed fine, but that was as much as she could say. In several of the preschool classrooms, children were sitting in front of a television watching cartoons, a passive arrangement that did not impress her. She met the teachers in the infant room, and they seemed kind and attentive. Most of the babies were not crying, and the teachers were attending to their needs as best as they could. Ten infants in the classroom seemed to be a lot for the two teachers to manage, but when Maria asked the director about the number of babies, the director assured her that the center was within the legal limit for the state.

Before filling out any paperwork, Maria asked to see the toddler room into which her son would graduate from the infant room. They approached the half-door to the room, and Maria immediately felt uncomfortable. There were three toddlers in the middle of the room fighting over a toy, and one of the toddlers bit the other two in an attempt to win the battle. While this fight was going on, Maria did not see an adult close to the children. She looked at the back of the classroom and saw a young teacher sitting on the floor and texting on her cell phone. The director looked extremely displeased. She asked Maria to please wait a moment, and she went into the classroom to speak to the teacher. Maria could see the two adults having an intense conversation. When the director joined Maria again, she had the teacher's cell phone in her hand and the teacher was sitting on the floor with the other children.

Although the director had handled the situation in the way that Maria would have wanted her to, the experience put a bad taste in her mouth.

Maria toured two other child-care programs that day. One was obviously a high-quality program, but it would cost four hundred dollars more per month than Maria and her husband could afford. No matter how much she wanted her son to attend that particular program, the tuition made it impossible. The program director told Maria about the state's child-care subsidy program that offered help for low-income families, but Maria and her husband would not qualify for a government-assistance program. Together the two of them made a comfortable salary, but with the new expenses of their first child, they could not afford one of the most expensive programs in the city. The third program that Maria toured did not meet their family's needs. The hours of operation would not allow her to work a full day at her job and pick up her son from child care before it closed.

After all the phone calls and tours, the first center that Maria had toured was the one program that she could afford and that would have a spot available at the end of her maternity leave. Other than the number of infants enrolled, she had liked the infant classroom and the teachers seemed caring. She would have concerns before her son graduated to the toddler room, but there was time to deal with that later. Maria decided that she would make an effort to communicate constantly with the teachers in her son's classroom, so that if there were any concerns they would hopefully let her know quickly. The program was only ten minutes away from their home, and they opened early enough that she would not have to be in a hurry to get to work on time.

When the day came for her son to start child care, Maria was much more emotional than she had anticipated. Not only was this the first time that she was leaving him with someone else for this amount of time, but it also was not the plan that she had anticipated. Leaving him with family had felt so much safer. Maria arrived at the center early so that she could bring in all of her son's diapers, wipes, and bottles. When she arrived, there were already eight babies in the classroom, and the two teachers were in the middle of giving bottles to two of the infants. There was no one who could hold her son as she attempted to leave him in child care for the first time. By the time Maria had put all of her son's personal items away, she knew that she needed to go. Maria placed her son in a bouncing seat, and one of the teachers bounced it with her foot as she fed another baby. Maria cried the entire way to work and throughout the morning.

The first month was extremely hard for Maria, even though the teachers continuously told her that it was harder for her than it was for her son. Maria began to watch to see if anyone was ever holding her son when she came to pick him up in the evenings.

He was always in a swing or a bouncing seat. It just seemed like there were too many infants in the classroom for him to get individualized attention at any point during the day. Maria called the expensive child-care program back at least twice to ask them questions about their policies. She looked at the family budget again and again to figure out how to cut back enough to pay for the expensive program, but it never seemed possible. Maria continually wondered how families with two (or more) children in child care could afford to place them in a program that didn't make them worry about their children's safety or comfort while the parents were at work. It seemed almost impossible.

Just after Maria's son turned six months old, Maria received a call at work from one of the centers where she had been added to the waiting list. A family was moving out of state, so the infant room at this program would have an opening in four weeks. The director wanted to know if Maria was still interested in enrolling her son. The cost would be $150 more per month than their current center, but Maria thought she and her husband might be able to come up with the additional money. She had not toured this facility before, so she thought that it was wise to visit it before deciding.

As soon as Maria arrived, she could tell this program was different. There was a security system at the front door to make sure that only families and employees could enter the facility. Maria also learned that there was a security camera set up in every room, and that parents received a password so they could observe their children's classrooms from a home or work computer during the day if they wanted to. This instantly made Maria believe that the teachers must be doing everything they were required to do, or they would not be so open to displaying the classrooms.

The director met Maria at the door and was friendly and personable. When she took Maria to see the infant classroom, Maria noticed immediately that there were only eight cribs in the room. One teacher was feeding a baby, and the other was sitting on the floor singing songs to the infants and playing peekaboo. Maria had never seen the teachers at her program have time to play with the infants. As they moved from room to room on the tour, Maria never saw a single adult on a cell phone. Each one of the teachers was talking to the children, leading a lesson, or assisting with hand washing. Artwork was displayed on the walls of even the classrooms of the youngest children. Although one or two children were occasionally crying during the tour, overall, the children seemed happy. Maria was stunned at the difference in the quality of care.

This center was farther away from their home and the cost was slightly more, but the difference in quality seemed significant. Maria had started to believe that a child-care program was only supposed to feed her son and set him back down in a safe place, because that is all that she had seen for the past four months. She was shocked when she saw what a child-care program could actually be. This was a center where she could leave her son during the day without crying or feeling guilty. She might be able to go to work and focus, knowing that he would be safe and happy.

Maria stayed at the center for another hour, filling out every piece of paperwork they gave her. She was a little bit worried about moving her son to a new program when he was accustomed to his current teachers. She and her husband had discussed how important it was to have a consistent school instead of moving from center to center if they became frustrated; however, this was completely different. They weren't moving because they were mad but because they had had no idea how much better a quality child-care program could be. This was a program her son could stay in until he started public school.

When Maria picked her son up from school that night, she let the director know that they would be leaving the center in three weeks. Maria took her son home and sat on the couch just holding him until it was time for bed. She finally felt at peace about his child care, and she couldn't help but wonder whether all the other families in his current child-care program knew about the other options for their children.

Chapter 6:
Child-Care Deserts

Finding quality child care is a challenging task for families, but it can be even harder when there is no child care from which to choose. Child-care programs all over the nation are having a difficult time maintaining financial stability, but there are some areas of the United States where no child-care programs are available. Often, programs have shut down because they could not bring in enough revenue to pay their bills. New businesses are not willing to take the same chance and lose their investment in starting a new program. That does not mean that there are not working families in those areas. Those families still need to work, and when faced with a lack of quality child care, they find any alternative so that they can maintain their jobs. These child-care deserts force parents to find poor quality care or to quit their jobs altogether to make sure that their children stay safe.

The Center for American Progress defines a *child-care desert* as an area with insufficient supply of licensed or regulated child-care programs based on the number of families in that area that need child care (Malik et al., 2018). Families who live in those communities must either drive outside the community to find care, find unregulated care that may not have mandatory health and safety requirements, or leave their jobs. None of these options is preferable. In 2018, 51 percent of Americans lived in an area described as a child-care desert (Malik et al., 2018).

Unfortunately, the typical laws of supply and demand do not seem to apply to child care. There is a huge demand for child care throughout the United States; however, adequate supply does not follow. This is because it costs more for a business to provide quality child care than parents are able to pay. When the business sets its rates low enough for parents to afford, the business becomes too financially vulnerable. At that point, any slight drop in enrollment or unexpected expenditure for facility costs can cause the business to close. Due to this fragile structure, 83 percent of parents report that finding affordable, quality child care is a problem (Malik et al., 2018). This is also why many parents report that child-care issues have a tendency to negatively affect their jobs.

Child-care deserts can be located anywhere. An entire town or county can be considered a child-care desert, but a desert can also be confined to one area of town, when the rest of the town may have ample options. The term *child-care desert* can also describe the entire landscape of child care in an area, or it can refer to specific subgroups of child care in an area. Several underserved groups of child care need more attention, including infant and toddler care, care for children with special needs, and child care during nontraditional hours.

The overall goal for quality child care in the United States comprises two separate components. First, child care needs to promote healthy child development and prepare young children to be successful when starting elementary school. Second, child care needs to provide a healthy and safe environment for children so that family members have the opportunity to participate in the workforce. When there is a distinct lack of child care in a large number of communities, it is not possible to achieve these goals.

The disparity between the cost of quality care and the available income of parents is the largest factor contributing to the vast number of child-care deserts in the United States (Malik et al., 2018). When a business is charging more for a service than the market will bear, typically that business will find ways to cut corners and make its service more affordable. For child care, the easiest ways to cut cost are lowering the wages of the staff members and placing more children into each classroom. In the field of child care, these are the exact cost-cutting measures that can compromise the very health and safety of the children being cared for. And it is not what the American public wants. Research shows that 92 percent of registered voters agree with increasing the health and safety quality in regulated child-care programs (Malik et al., 2018). So instead of reducing quality to make child-care programs more available, America must generate financially sustainable programs to care for its children. This means that systemic change is needed.

RURAL VERSUS URBAN ACCESS

Communities are often viewed as either rural or urban. Based on information from the US Census Bureau, communities can be categorized into three different categories: urban, suburban, and rural (Malik and Hamm, 2017). Each of these different types of communities has the potential to be a child-care desert without enough regulated child care to serve the working families in that area. Even with the three distinct categories of communities, rural areas encounter the greatest number of child-care deserts. Almost three out of five rural communities (59 percent) are considered child-care deserts (Malik et al., 2018).

In rural communities, it is most common to utilize family child-care homes. Because these homes typically enroll six to twelve children, the number of children served in the community is significantly smaller than it would be if the predominant form of child care were in child-care centers. The main reason that center-based child care is harder to support in rural areas is that homes are frequently spaced far apart, and geographic proximity to child care can be a challenge to filling all the spots available in a center (Malik et al., 2018).

High-income suburban neighborhoods are the most likely to have an ample supply of child care (Malik et al., 2018). Regulated child-care programs, both licensed centers and family child-care homes, are more likely to open in suburban areas because families who live in those neighborhoods are most likely to pay the required tuition. Child-care deserts can still be found in suburban neighborhoods, but they are most likely specific to underserved populations, such as infant and toddler care and child care for children with special needs (Malik et al., 2018).

In urban areas, child-care deserts are still more common than you might anticipate. Research shows that 56 percent of urban areas show significant gaps in necessary child care (Malik et al., 2018). Families frequently use family child-care homes because the cost of renting or buying building space in urban areas may be a significant expense for child-care centers. This means that many family child-care homes are in apartments or small condos, and room for children may be limited by the square footage of the space. Another obstacle for urban family child-care homes can be that neighbors and landlords may not approve of a small business operating within the home or with a small group of children making noise that may disturb other tenants.

Particularly in rural and urban settings, where center-based child care is significantly limited, families may turn to neighbors to watch their children when they cannot find regulated child care. While it is very generous for a neighbor to offer this type of service, it is still important to remember that the neighbor still needs to demonstrate adherence to the essential health and safety standards that are required in other child-care options. One safety requirement that can often be skipped in neighbor care is a background check. Families may feel that it is rude to request a background check from an acquaintance who has offered to help the family, but it is still the family's top priority to make sure that the children are safe from illness, injuries, abuse, and neglect. It can be easy for the family to assume that a child is safe because the neighbor seems kind and dependable, but without knowing more about the child-care provider's full background, that assumption is a potentially dangerous one to make.

UNDERSERVED POPULATIONS

There are specific groups of children for whom not enough child care is available, regardless of the community in which they live. These populations include infants and toddlers, children with disabilities, and children who need care during nontraditional hours. The number of child-care centers that serve these populations is limited for several reasons. Each of these types of care is more expensive for child-care providers and, in turn, for families. These populations may require that the center seek amendments to the child-care license so that they may offer that type of care. Finally, there may not be enough families who need this type of care and live nearby for the center to enroll the necessary number of children.

Infants and Toddlers

Child care for infants and toddlers is much harder to find than that for children who are three years of age or older (Malik et al., 2018). There are specific financial reasons for this shortage. Infant and toddler classrooms have smaller adult-to-child ratios, so they automatically cost the child-care program more to staff. In turn, child-care programs must charge more, and families may not be able to afford those additional fees. This cost difference can be a significant burden for first-time parents who have never had to pay child-care expenses before, and they must find a way to trim their budgets to accommodate the one thousand dollars or more per month required for their child's care.

Despite the need for high-quality care in the infant and toddler years, teachers of those age groups are paid approximately two dollars per hour less than preschool teachers (Malik et al., 2018). A lack of pay equality for our infant-toddler teachers shows that they are not valued as highly as our preschool teachers. If the teachers for the littlest children are not shown respect, they will look for jobs or careers where they feel more valued. That might mean that a teacher is initially hired as an infant teacher but attempts to move to a higher-paying classroom as soon as possible when an opening becomes available. It could also mean that a teacher is hired because she loves working with infants, but she becomes discouraged and leaves the field completely. Babies and toddlers need to develop secure attached relationships as the foundation for their emotional development as they grow (Honig, 2014). High turnover in infant and toddler classrooms interferes with formation of attachment to a consistent, loving caregiver.

When the cost of center-based care seems too overwhelming, parents will often try to reduce the cost by patching together different child-care arrangements for each day. For example, the mother may watch the child on Mondays and Wednesdays, the father on Tuesdays, a grandmother on Thursdays, and a neighbor on Fridays. This type of inconsistent care makes it difficult for the baby to establish attached relationships, experience a consistent schedule, and benefit from language-rich environments; all of this taken together amounts to poor-quality care. However, if a patchwork of care is the only option the family can afford, they may not have other alternatives.

Children with Special Needs

Another underserved population in child-care programs comprises children with special needs. Given the many different special needs and disabilities that a child can experience, it can be hard to place all these children into one category. A child with a slight delay in speech articulation may simply need to be in a classroom setting where she hears other children using appropriate pronunciation and has opportunities to practice. Other children may need significantly more support. Children diagnosed with diabetes or epilepsy, for example, need a teacher who feels comfortable administering medication or first aid. Children with challenging behaviors created by anxiety, autism, or sensory-processing disorder may need individualized attention and supports throughout the day, placing a much greater demand on the caregiver and child-care program.

Many child-care centers and family child-care homes are not equipped to support children with special needs and offer them high-quality care. One of the greatest challenges for child-care providers is the lack of training on specific disabilities or medical conditions, so they do not know the best way to care for a child with special needs. The public school system can offer training from special educators that can help a teacher learn how best to support these children in their classrooms. Child-care programs, on the other hand, rarely have a specialist on staff who can offer this type of training. Moreover, the classroom may not be equipped to support the child. For example, if a child frequently needs time alone after becoming overstimulated in a group setting, a classroom or home filled with other young children may lack sufficient space for this type of necessary accommodation.

Another challenge in supporting and caring for children with special needs is the required adult-to-child ratio. All regulated child-care programs must meet a minimum state-mandated adult-to-child ratio. Of course, high-quality child-care programs will often lower that ratio to give the children more individualized attention. Not all programs have the financial stability to do that. If a child-care program has two teachers in a room of twenty-four preschoolers, it can be very challenging to support the classroom as a whole and simultaneously support a child with special needs who requires a great deal of individualized care. This can lead to safety concerns for all the children in the classroom, if there is not enough supervision to keep all children safe.

Many child-care programs that focus on serving the general population of young children can unintentionally set up their center policies to be inhospitable to children with disabilities. For example, centers may have a policy that states that all children must be toilet-trained before moving from the toddler classrooms to the preschool classrooms. For children developing at or above the typical developmental rate, these policies would not be an issue; however, they can be problematic for children with disabilities. A child with autism may not be developmentally ready to use the toilet independently until the age of five or six. Does that mean that child must stay in the toddler room for the remainder of his time at the child-care program? Or will the program dismiss him when he reaches age three because he cannot meet the expectations of the preschool classroom?

Children with disabilities can be challenged by toilet-training policies, biting policies, and other policies addressing other challenging behaviors. For centers that focus their policies toward typically developing children, these policies can often lead to children with special needs being suspended or expelled much more frequently than other students. Suspension and expulsion from child care can have a huge impact on the entire family. A young child can suffer socially and emotionally from being removed abruptly from a familiar setting. Parents may have to scramble to find alternative child care to maintain a job, but many parents of children with special needs may have to resign from their jobs if specialized care is not available in their area.

Children Who Need Care during Nontraditional Hours

Communities throughout the United States also lack child care for families who work nights and weekends. Many child-care programs are only open during daytime hours, most commonly 6:00 a.m. to 6:00 p.m. Only 8 percent of child-care centers and approximately one-third of family child-care homes watch children during nights and weekends (Malik et al., 2018). This lack of care is particularly hard for low-income families, 58 percent of whom have at least one parent who works between 6:00 p.m. and 8:00 a.m. (Malik et al., 2018).

For child-care centers, it can be extremely expensive to keep a building open for extended hours when only a small number of families need these additional services. Both centers and family child-care homes need additional resources to offer this type of care, including additional beds and hygiene supplies, as well as funding to cover the additional utilities costs. Family child-care homes are much more likely to offer night and weekend care; however, the most common source of nontraditional child care is family, friend, and neighbor (FFN) care. This type of care is typically license-exempt care, which means a child-care license is not required, depending on the number of children who are cared for in the home. FFN care can potentially receive state child-care-subsidy funding, depending on how the state sets its minimal standards. FFN care is definitely an asset for night and evening care; however, it still does not meet the nationwide need for families who work nontraditional hours, particularly families with low incomes.

DECLINE OF FAMILY CHILD-CARE HOMES

A family child-care home is a child-care provider that cares for small groups of children in a residential building, such as a house, apartment, or condo (Office of Child Care, 2019). The regulations for family child-care homes vary from state to state. Depending on the state, a family child-care home may need to be licensed. Also, depending on the state, the care may or may not be in the home in which the child-care provider lives. Licensed or regulated family child care must meet minimum health and safety guidelines, including background checks of the provider and anyone else who lives in the home with the provider. Regulations also require regular inspections of the family child-care home to ensure that it meets that state's minimum standards. A less formal type of family child care is FFN care. This type of care is typically license-exempt, but the providers are more limited in the number of children they are allowed to care for.

Family child-care homes can have several benefits not offered in child-care centers. They usually serve six to twelve children at once, so some families really appreciate the smaller group size and family atmosphere. Also, because the children are cared for in one space, siblings have the opportunity to be together during the day instead of being separated into age-specific classrooms as they would be in center-based care. Family child-care homes have a great deal of flexibility in when they offer child care, so they can be an important source of evening and weekend care for families who work nontraditional hours. Finally, family child-care homes can be more appealing to families, because they may be less expensive than typical center-based care.

Despite the benefits of family child-care homes, there has been a significant decrease in this type of child care. Between 2005 and 2017, 97,000 family child-care homes closed throughout the United States (Office of Child Care, 2019). This decrease in family child care created challenges for vulnerable and low-income families, including those who work nontraditional hours, who live in rural communities, who need infant or toddler care, or who do not speak English as their primary language. Many families prefer family child-care homes because it is much easier for in-home child care to meet the cultural needs of the families, particularly those who do not speak English.

Despite the need for family child-care homes, the list of reasons why such large numbers of these care arrangements have closed is significant. Due to economic cuts, 336,000 family child-care providers lost subsidies between 2005 to 2017 (National Center on Early Childhood Quality Assurance [NCECQA], 2019). Many family child-care homes specifically serve families with low incomes, so when those families no longer qualify for a subsidy, a child-care provider does not receive enough income to keep his business open. These providers work in a field with low and unpredictable income, and they receive no benefits as small-business owners. Many choose this profession because they deeply care for the children and families in their communities; however, if they can't generate enough income to pay their bills, they must consider a drastic career change.

Another obstacle is that many in-home child-care providers do not have the business expertise to keep their businesses running efficiently. They must know how to set up a budget, how to set their rates to cover their costs, and how to file their taxes appropriately. If they struggle to complete these basic skills, then their businesses can lose money instead of making a profit. An additional challenge for these businesses throughout the United States is local zoning laws. Many counties maintain zoning laws that prohibit storefront businesses from opening in neighborhood settings. Unfortunately, those laws can affect family child care also. The point of family child care is that it operates in the home with a small group of children, but if the laws prevent a family child-care home from opening in a residential neighborhood, the county is significantly limiting the child-care options of its working families.

Many family child-care home providers have been working in this business for decades. Some are now serving the children of students that they had in their homes years ago. Family child care, like all child care, is a demanding field. It requires providers to work long hours, and its many physical demands include lifting children for diaper changes and moving them in and out of cribs. Spending all day with young children instead of being around other adults can also make an adult feel isolated. After decades of this hard work, many men and women who work in this field are approaching retirement, but new providers are not following in their footsteps. Younger generations of child-care providers are joining centers rather than opening their own family child-care homes. In order to preserve this style of child care and support underserved areas, it is essential to increase recruitment for in-home child-care professionals.

A LOOK AT APPALACHIA

Louise has worked as a child-care resource specialist and a child-care advocate in Appalachia for the majority of her career. In the mountains, families are often spaced very far apart, and resources may not be readily available. In her role, Louise has tried to recruit additional child-care providers and support those members of the community who are already providing child care. Due to distance or financial instability, the significant lack of center-based child care in this area forces most families to turn to in-home child care.

Louise and her colleagues work hard to recruit child-care providers to become regulated; however, many of them do not see the need to adhere to additional requirements. The most common type of care in the area is FFN care. Family and friends usually charge the families they serve much less than a licensed center would, and the lower cost is based on relationships between the families and the caregiver. Supporting others in the community is a strong Appalachian cultural value. Many of the same families have lived in these communities for generations, so the families all know one another.

In more densely populated areas, Louise believes there may be more middle-income families who desire center-based care for their children, but to keep the center profitable, at least half of the enrollment would have to come from low-income families. That means that the cost of care would still be governed to some extent by a child-care subsidy reimbursement program. Although many families might qualify for a subsidy, often the amount cannot cover the full cost of tuition, especially for infant and toddler care. If a family does not have the ability to pay the overage cost above their subsidy, they will be unable to use a center-based program, and another child-care center is at risk of closing if it cannot reach full enrollment.

When a family cannot find a consistent source of child care so that the adults can work, Louise often sees them attempt to create a patchwork of child care that can result in inconsistency for the young children. This type of puzzle happens just as frequently in response to a lack of options as it does for families who cannot pay the high cost of center-based care.

Although Louise and her colleagues work hard to explain to child-care providers the benefits of being a regulated family child-care home, many of the people in the area are not interested. A large number of providers are caring for a family member, and they do not see the need to meet a series of requirements to do the same job they are already doing, particularly if they believe that the arrangement is temporary. Others may not want a state official coming into their homes and grading them on how well they are doing their job. They may be apprehensive of any type of government involvement. Some providers are concerned about the additional costs they would incur due to zoning permits or increases to their homeowner's insurance. Finally, there is a small group of providers who may be apprehensive about their background checks or the background checks of other family members who live in their homes. Louise frequently finds that the child-care providers who are interested in becoming regulated have previously worked in some type of child care, such as center-based care, so they are more familiar with the regulations and less likely to be skeptical about the process.

Because of a lack of economic development in Appalachia, large numbers of young children qualify to attend Head Start and Early Head Start. Early Head Start is not available in every community, but it is available in most. Louise strongly believes that the Head Start programs in her area do an amazing job of recruiting families and enrolling them into their programs. The largest barrier for Head Start is that they have had to centralize some of their programs that cover multiple communities, so some young children may have very long bus rides to and from school. This makes some families less willing to participate, even if they qualify. The other barrier for Head Start is that the hours of service may not work for many families. If a Head Start program provides only half-day services, the family will still need to find child care for the remainder of the work day, leading to inconsistent routines and schedules for the children.

Head Start programs rate as some of the highest quality programs in Louise's state, so the children who attend Head Start get access to quality early education. Outside of Head Start, many families may not be aware of what quality child care looks like, since most families are just looking for access to child care. The public school system in Louise's state offers a developmental screening to each child before he or she enters kindergarten. The results of the screenings are used to help the school system estimate how many of the new kindergarten students are "ready for school" according to the screening tool. The lack of quality child-care options for the communities Louise serves can easily be seen in the results of the kindergarten screening. That lack is even more obvious when the results are compared with those of the communities in suburban areas that have ample access to high-quality child care.

Many resources are lacking throughout Appalachia, but quality child care should be considered essential to developing the community. If families have more access to quality child care, they will be able to obtain consistent, higher-paying jobs that could break the poverty cycle. And consistent child care will support child development and prepare children for elementary school.

To obtain high-quality care for the community, Louise believes that several different supports are needed. First, the child-care subsidy amount must be increased to cover the full cost of child care, so that low-income families will not have to pay a significant overage fee, particularly for infant and toddler care. Second, the rural communities need additional supports for mentoring programs and technical assistance to recruit more child-care providers and train them in developmentally appropriate practice. Finally, the business community throughout Appalachia needs a better understanding of how consistent child care would assist their businesses and how the business community could support the supply-and-demand issues surrounding child care. To enable the rural areas to offer the child care needed for the families who live there, additional supports and resources must be made available.

Chapter 7:
Impact on the
Business Community

To be able to hold a job, parents must have reliable child care. In the absence of consistent, quality child care, it is not only the working families who suffer; the business community also suffers. Sixty-five percent of parents state that their work schedule has been affected by child-care challenges by an average of seven and a half days per six-month time period (CCA, 2019). Research from the annual report of Child Care Aware of America (2019) states that an annual economic loss of $57 billion in earnings, productivity, and revenue can be traced back to the child-care crisis.

Businesses can see a significant difference when they assist employees with access to quality child care through a network or by providing on-site child care. CCA of America (2019) states that 54 percent of employers discovered that access to child care services reduced employees' time off by 30 percent, and on-site child care reduced staff turnover up to 60 percent. This type of improvement benefits the families as much as the businesses, since parents in the United States can lose between $30 and $35 billion in household income annually due to a reduction of work hours or leaving the workforce completely (Gould and Blair, 2020).

THE STATE AND NATIONAL PERSPECTIVES

In the past several years, many individual states have made a special effort to research how a lack of child care may be affecting their state's economy. One of the first studies of this kind came out of Louisiana. Louisiana State University's Public Policy Research Lab surveyed families with children ages four and under throughout the state to see how a lack of child care affects them. Half the respondents in the survey stated that they rely on a family member for some amount of child care (Davis et al., 2017). One of every six respondents had quit a job due to lack of consistent child care, and one out of every thirteen respondents had been fired due to persistent problems with child care (Davis et al., 2017). More than 40 percent of respondents reported missing work in the previous three months due to issues with child care. During the twelve months prior to the survey, the Louisiana economy lost $816 million due to absences and employee turnover related to child care, and there was a total of $1.1 billion of economic loss for Louisiana related to child care as a whole (Davis et al., 2017).

Indiana conducted a similar workforce study in 2018. The results indicated that lack of child care created an annual loss of $1.1 billion in economic activity for the twelve months leading up to the research study (Littlepage, 2018). The results also showed an annual loss of $118.8 million in tax revenue and an annual loss of $1.8 billion in direct cost to employers (Littlepage, 2018). Georgia's workforce study in 2018 yielded similar results. The surveys showed that Georgia suffered an annual loss of $1.75 billion in overall economic loss and an additional $105 million in lost tax revenue (Goldberg et al., 2018). That means that Georgia's economy could have been almost $2 billion stronger with consistent child care.

In 2018, a nationwide research study was conducted by Clive Belfield, an economics professor from New York, with funding from the Pritzker Children's Initiative. This study included responses from 812 working parents who had children ages three and under. Again, the survey showed large-scale economic loss when families are unable to work due to a lack of child care. The survey showed that working parents lose an average of $3,350 annually in reduced productivity at work (Belfield, 2018). Multiplying that loss by 11 million parents in the US workforce leads to an annual loss of $37 billion (Belfield, 2018). Businesses lose an average of $1,150 annually per working parent in reduced revenue and recruiting costs for a total of $13 billion each year (Belfield, 2018). Finally, the research showed that taxpayers lose an average of $630 annually per working parent in lower income tax and sales tax for a total of $6.9 billion annually (Belfield, 2018).

Belfield's national survey also found interesting points that were not addressed in the state research studies. For example, Belfield's 2018 study found that the average parent lost two hours of work time per week (approximately 5 percent of paid time) due to child-care problems. Also, more than half of working parents said that they are late to work, miss a full or half day of work, or are distracted at work due to issues with child care (Belfield, 2018).

The surveys definitely showed how parents' careers suffer from inconsistent child care. Twenty-five percent of parents stated that they had to reduce their work hours or turn down job offers due to child-care limitations (Belfield, 2018). One in every six parents stated that they had to turn down a promotion due to lack of child care, and one in every seven stated that their pay or their number of work hours had to be reduced before they eventually quit (Belfield, 2018). Consistent child care would allow parents to avoid damage to their careers and would prevent child care–related financial loss to the families, businesses, and communities.

THE BENEFITS OF CHILD CARE FOR BUSINESSES

Employers have the opportunity to support working parents in a variety of ways. Providing on-site child care is one way to help employees come to work more consistently (and reduce staff turnover), but it is not the only way to help staff members with child care. Employers can offer to subsidize child-care expenses for employees or create a network of child-care providers that can prioritize the company's families over the general public. These types of benefits can have many positive effects.

Employees with company-assisted child care can enjoy longer tenure with their employers, and the companies can face less turnover. One way the employers can see this is by examining the careers of working mothers. Most mothers are now older and closer to mid-career when they begin having children (Bui and Miller, 2018). Since they are no longer entry-level employees when they have their children, they have developed greater worth to the employer. If a mother decides not to return from her maternity leave due to lack of child care, that decision can cost the company a great deal of money to recruit and train another employee to replace a veteran employee in mid-career.

Consistent child care can also enhance employee performance. When a parent is worried about a child, it can be very challenging for her to focus on the task at hand, at work or anywhere. However, when parents feel that their children are safe, they are less likely to worry and more capable of focusing entirely on their assigned tasks. Higher performance can also be related to consistent attendance. Parents without reliable child care frequently must stay home from work to provide child care themselves, which can lead to poor performance with delayed deadlines and other team members assuming more than their share of the workload. Reliable, employer-assisted child care can alleviate many of those concerns.

In the current business climate, potential employees are comparing benefit packages as well as salaries when they receive a job offer. Many millennial employees look at the benefits package and fringe benefits of the job just as closely as the salary (Power, 2019). Health insurance and paid time off are standard employee benefits, but unique benefits such as employer-assisted child care can give some companies the edge when it comes to recruiting new talent. Employers that look at the needs of their employees and find benefits that meet their situation in life can gain access to a larger talent pool simply by showing interest in their employees' lives. These types of benefits can raise the morale of staff by showing them that they are supported in a family-friendly workplace. This approach is especially appealing now that more women are in management positions and more fathers are actively engaged in their children's lives.

REOPENING BUSINESSES AFTER COVID-19

As of this writing, the COVID-19 pandemic has had a devastating effect on the child-care industry, along with many other industries. Many states have required that child-care programs limit the number of children who can be served in their facilities, to maintain social distance and prevent the rapid spread of the virus among the children and the employees in the programs. Because COVID-19 has significantly limited the number of children who can be served in child care, it has limited the workforce as a whole.

In the spring of 2020, when many states limited the businesses and industries that were open to those that focused on serving essential employees, this lack of child care did not seem to be as devastating because many businesses asked all employees to work from home whenever possible. Child-care programs and public schools were not open for face-to-face care, but children could be at home during the day with their families, so the need for child care was not as significant as it would be if the workforce were completely open.

This does not mean that working parents did not face challenges during this time period. Homes were turned into makeshift child-care programs and schools. Many families enjoyed the initial arrangements because they were no longer commuting to work and could spend more time with their families. After several weeks, however, the families fully absorbed the reality of the increase in workload. Parents were attempting to do a full day of work while also assisting school-age children with online learning and providing constant supervision to younger children. Stress levels dramatically increased for working families. Adults balanced a full day of meetings and assignments with intermittent breaks for online learning, preparing meals, mediating fights between siblings, and keeping the home environment safe.

In many households, the additional workload fell predominantly on the mothers (Stanton, 2020). With multiple hours each day being devoted to the care and education of the children, mothers were trying to complete their work responsibilities early in the morning or late into the evening, leaving little time to care for their own personal needs. As exhaustion and increasing workloads created a heavy burden, many mothers and single parents faced the question of possibly reducing their hours at work or resigning their positions altogether. This type of economic impact will continue to be felt long past the distribution of the vaccine for COVID-19.

The Bureau of Labor Statistics estimates that, in two-thirds of two-parent families, both parents work. In addition, there are 13.6 million single-parent homes (Stanton, 2020). If a large portion of these parents leave the workforce, significant economic impacts will follow. Even leaving the workforce for two to three years can have a profound financial impact on a family and set the parent back several years in seniority, as well as limiting the upward mobility through the parent's entire career (Stanton, 2020). Women who reduce their working hours, work part time, decline promotions, and so on to care for their families limit their careers over time (Stanton, 2020). Initially, small career choices that allow more flexibility for a young family may not seem significant. By the time a woman is approaching retirement, however, she is able to see exactly how far she has distanced herself from her male colleagues by making choices affected by child-care issues.

Another economic factor to consider is that two-income families have made decisions over time that are supported by those two incomes. They have purchased homes and cars that are within the budget of the dual-income lifestyle, along with costs of necessary services such as child care. If the collapse of child care requires one parent to resign a position to care for the children, then the family is automatically at risk of losing their home or having to declare bankruptcy when they cannot pay necessary bills. Of course, with planning, a family can downsize their home and expenses; however, the sudden onset of the COVID-19 pandemic did not allow for planning. Child-care programs were closed. Jobs were lost. Families had to adjust as quickly as possible. Some families had emergency savings to support them for a limited amount of time, but the pandemic was not a limited event. As the crisis continued, families were more at risk. The need for family supports such as unemployment insurance and government-support programs such as SNAP increased, and families were left with few resources.

The truth is that the United States cannot have a functioning economy without a stable child-care system. Even if families do not want their children to return to group child care until after a vaccine is widely available, the system needs to remain in place for long-term recovery (Stanton, 2020). If the United States allows the system to erode while many parents are still working from home, then many parents will not be able to return to face-to-face employment. Even if many employees continue to work remotely as a permanent change, it is challenging for a parent to be productive at her job while also having to care for and supervise a young child at the same time. The child-care industry serves an essential role, and it should be categorized as an essential business.

In her interview with Zach Stanton of *Politico* magazine, Betsey Stevenson, a renowned economist, questions the federal government's choice to support and offer financial compensation to other essential businesses instead of fully supporting the child-care industry (Stanton, 2020). She is amazed that the government and so many businesses still see child care as a personal problem for families. Many other issues that were once seen as personal problems have been re-evaluated over time; for example, when the United States recognized the devastating effects of a lack of health care, the government created Medicare (Stanton, 2020). K-12 education was deemed important enough that it was made mandatory for children, and the federal and state government systems began to support education more. Unfortunately, the early childhood education system has never received the same traction.

> **"Child care is not a personal issue, it's not a women's issue; it's actually an economic issue."**
>
> **—Betsey Stevenson, economist**

During the pandemic, other industries were deemed essential and given a great deal more support than the child-care system. The nationwide airline industry, for example, received a large amount of financial assistance in the COVID-19 aid packages from the federal government, even though the pandemic seriously limited the ability of Americans to fly. The government took this stance because the long-term loss of America's airlines would have a devastating impact on business and tourism, debilitating the American economy. Stevenson points out that the loss of child care in the United States could have a larger impact than the airline system on the national economy, yet the entire child-care system received less funding than that given to a single airline company—Delta (Stanton, 2020).

The collapse of the child-care industry would have long-term effects that could debilitate the economy for years to come. Stevenson says an investment in child care is an investment in the overall health and well-being of our children, as well as an investment in support of the workforce (Stanton, 2020). As child-care programs close or reduce capacity, higher-income families may still be able to hire private child care for their children; however, lower-income families will be unable to make that choice. The gap between socioeconomic groups will only continue to grow. Research from the National Center for Education Statistics shows that one in five children living in poverty utilizes center-based child care (Fraga, 2019). The collapse of regulated child care in centers or in family child-care homes will make it even harder for low- and middle-income families to obtain child care.

A middle-income family in which one parent loses a job due to lack of child care can easily become a low-income family. In 2019, the Committee for Economic Development (CED) reported that 15 million children are in some type of paid child care (2019). If the United States loses the estimated 40 percent of child-care programs that NAEYC estimated at the onset of the pandemic (NAEYC, 2020), how many members of the workforce will the US economy lose? Some of these families will look for nontraditional child-care options; however, the pandemic has also decreased these options. Before the pandemic, many families relied on grandparents to watch children while the parents were at work, but fewer families are choosing this option due to the additional health risks for older people if exposed to the COVID-19 virus (Stanton, 2020). This means that many families have the difficult choice between leaving young children at home alone in an attempt to maintain a job and salary needed to support the family financially or deciding to function on the income of one parent while the other parent cares for the children.

One final economic perspective to consider is that shutting down child-care programs leaves many Americans without jobs provided through the child-care industry itself. The US Chamber of Commerce Foundation stated in August 2020 that more than 700,000 child-care programs nationwide are in danger of closing, due to the economic uncertainty brought on by the COVID-19 pandemic. Many of these programs are small businesses that belong to their local chamber of commerce. These businesses provide not only child care but also jobs. More Americans will be seeking unemployment benefits as child-care programs continue to close.

THE EMPLOYER PERSPECTIVE

Kevin works in an urban area where he manages nine medical clinics. His company has sites throughout the United States and employs approximately 50,000 workers. At his set of clinics, Kevin supervises approximately 100 employees, about 30 percent of whom are dependent on child care so they can be at work. Because Kevin works in the medical industry, it is essential to have employees who are well trained, not only with medical degrees but also in the specific patient population with which they work each day. Overall, the company offers a variety of benefits to attract qualified employees, including health, dental, and vision insurance; paid time off; extended sick leave; and a matching 401(k) plan for retirement. At this time, it does not offer specific child-care benefits.

Considering that 30 percent of the employees on Kevin's staff need consistent child care, the topic has come up frequently. Many of his employees report to work between 4 and 5 a.m., a factor that makes it challenging for them to obtain child care. Almost no child-care programs in the area open that early. While some employees have a spouse or family member who can stay with their children until the child-care program or elementary school opens in the morning, single parents struggle to find child care that suits their schedule. When previously arranged child care falls through, many employees must take time off. That can be very challenging for a business that must have a specific number of trained professionals at work each day to offer the necessary medical services to patients.

Kevin's employees not only struggle with availability; the cost of child care is also an onerous burden for them. Despite the fact that the majority of Kevin's staff are medical professionals, many do not earn high salaries. Medical assistants, nutritionists, phlebotomists, and other medical technicians may struggle with the cost of child care, especially if they have more than one child who needs full-time or even part-time child care. Their low incomes lead many employees to look for care in family child-care homes or other nontraditional care settings rather than the more expensive center-based settings. Unfortunately, nontraditional care is often less reliable than regulated child care, leading more employees to have to take time off due to child-care problems. Kevin also has seen employees struggle to stay focused at work because they are worried about their children not being in a quality child-care setting or because they are worried about their older elementary or young middle-school students being independent at home and getting themselves on the school bus in the morning. In the medical field, the reliability of the staff is crucial. Consistent child care is essential to enabling the entire workforce to be present and focused.

Kevin believes that one reason the company has never addressed the issue of child care is the size of the business. With 50,000 employees nationwide, it would be very difficult to set up child-care discounts or benefits in multiple states. Before the pandemic, because Kevin had not had one of his team members ask for on-site child care or child-care benefits, he had not discussed the topic with human resources. Although, in the past, Kevin has had employees resign because they wanted to stay home with a new baby or because they could not find consistent child care that fit the company schedule, he never really saw this as a business issue. The percentage of employees who resigned was not exceptionally high, and parents have a right to decide who is best to care for their children.

Now, however, when he sits down to analyze the cost in dollars and time of training a new employee to fill an opening, he realizes that the cost is significant. By the time Kevin posts a position, interviews candidates, onboards the new hire, and trains the employee on the new position, there can be a staffing gap of four to five months. That is a definite loss of productivity and a strain on company resources.

Only five to ten employees at any one clinic need child care, so creating an on-site program would not be financially justifiable. The need for full-time child care at a single clinic would not match the cost of the facility or the staffing that the child-care program would require. Still, the lack of child care in the early morning hours has been a reason for losing potential employees in the past. The company is always looking to hire the best talent for these positions, and salaries are becoming more competitive at many of the other clinics in the area. If the pay is similar, what would stop a qualified employee from going to a clinic that opens at a more reasonable hour?

The limited availability of child care during the pandemic changed Kevin's viewpoint quite a bit. In March 2020, Kevin's state initially limited child-care programs to serving essential employees only. Kevin's employees were considered essential, but many child-care programs were temporarily closing their doors, because serving only essential employees did not provide enough income to cover the costs of operation. The child-care programs that were open increased their charges so that they could cover their fixed costs with limited enrollment.

It was at this time that many of Kevin's employees with young children considered taking leaves of absence. Their children's elementary schools were closed, and the cost of child care had become a significant financial burden. Nonessential medical procedures were being limited, but regular services such as dialysis would continue throughout the pandemic regardless of the state of emergency. Kevin needed to make sure that he kept enough qualified employees working during the pandemic restrictions to conduct these necessary medical procedures, and he did not want to lose exemplary staff who felt unsupported by the company.

Kevin's clinics were not the only ones in the company that began to feel the strain. Many areas of the country suffered due to lack of child care, so the corporate office had to figure out how to keep its clinics open until the economy stabilized. The executive team decided to offer a significant financial subsidy to employees paying for child care. If employees brought in their receipts for weekly child-care tuition, the receipts would be submitted to the corporate office for reimbursement.

This subsidy made it possible for many employees to continue to work during the state of emergency, but cost was not the only problem. The company's early hours of operation often required family members, particularly grandparents, to watch young children before child-care programs' typical hours of operation. Since the at-risk population for the COVID-19 virus included those individuals who are sixty years of age or older and those with pre-existing medical conditions, many employees who were willing to work during the pandemic asked for schedule changes so they could come into work when the child-care programs were open.

It became obvious to Kevin that there was a great need in his area for child-care programs that not only offered care for children from 6 a.m. to 6 p.m. but also offered extended hours. Kevin tried to rearrange schedules for employees as he could, but several employees ended up having to stay at home with their children even after the company offered to subsidize the cost of child care. These staff members were very concerned about how long the state of emergency would last, because they did not know how long their family could afford to give up one salary. Kevin was worried that if the family found a way to live without that salary, then a well-trained employee may not want to return to work. That departure could potentially leave him with multiple openings at once and the inability to serve all his patients.

He learned that there were at least two centers in the area that were open twenty-four hours per day, but his employees told him that these were not quality programs so they did not want to leave their children there. Other employees said that they typically had left their children in family child-care homes, because the in-home providers were willing to be more flexible with their hours. However, due to their own health risks, many of those providers were temporarily closed during the state of emergency. Kevin realized that finding the care that they needed for their children was a challenge for these working parents.

Kevin's employees were not the only ones who struggled. Lots of restaurants, retail establishments, hospitals, and factories had employees who worked second or third shifts and weekends. Where were those employees able to find safe child care for their children? Kevin realized that people needed more options, not just during the pandemic but as a long-term solution.

Chapter 8:
The Link between Child Care and the Public School System

The public school system is the largest source of education and supervision of children in the United States. All children are eligible for a public school education, and the system does an excellent job of providing the accommodations that children need to have the most appropriate education for their individual developmental levels. Policies and procedures for public schools do vary from state to state, since each state has the ability to create its own set of requirements for the school system; however, the overall foundation of the school system is consistent throughout the country. Along with special-education services to help children receive an appropriate education, the public school system also provides resources such as mental-health services and resource centers to support all of the children and families who attend.

Although the public school system offers a variety of learning opportunities and supports for all of the children enrolled, working families may need additional assistance. The public school system does not typically provide the supervision for a working parent to complete a full work week while children are being taught by qualified educators. Families often need additional child care from private child-care programs, in addition to the services offered through the public school system, to make sure that the family has all the supports possible to be successful.

AFTER-SCHOOL CARE FOR SCHOOL-AGE CHILDREN

Children who attend a K-12 school system typically attend school for thirty hours per week, ten hours less than the amount of time a working parent attends a full-time job. This means that parents who work full time outside of the home usually need an additional 13.5 hours of care each week (including their travel time) to ensure their children are in a safe environment while they are apart from their parents (Adam and Todd, 2020). Research shows that the national average cost of after-school child care for one child is between $100 and $125 per week, depending on the type of program the family uses (Adam and Todd, 2020). After-school care offered at a public school building is typically less expensive than a private child-care program that sends a van to the school to pick the children up once the school day is complete. At the same time, public school programs for after school are limited in size and availability.

The Afterschool Alliance (2014) states that 50 percent of school-age children need after-school child care, whether that need is met or unmet. The organization also asserts that for every child who successfully obtains a spot in an after-school program, there are two more children waiting for a spot to open. The demand for after-school child care far exceeds the supply, but families can choose from a variety of options. Many licensed child-care centers have a school-age classroom available for care after the elementary school day and for full-day care in the summers. Family child-care homes may also provide after-school care for children between the ages of six and thirteen. Some families may prefer this option because children from the same family can more easily stay together in care, and family child-care homes can offer flexible hours of care during nights and weekends. Some businesses, such as after-school karate camps and dance classes, may offer license-exempt child care for older students, in which the children can learn a skill while waiting for their parents to get off work. Family care is still a very popular option, if grandparents or other family members live in the area. Finally, as children reach the middle-school age range, more children may be able to care for themselves independently after the bus drops them off at home.

Even with a variety of options, the Afterschool Alliance (2014) cites that 11.3 million school-age children are without care from 3 to 6 p.m. daily, due to the gap between the school day and the parents' work schedules. When families who use school-age care were asked about its importance, 83 percent of parents said they must have after-school care in order to keep their jobs (Afterschool Alliance, 2014). Because children have already participated in seven hours of structured learning during the school day, parents do not typically have the same expectations of after-school care as they do for child care for children from birth to age five. Most parents are looking for a safe and clean environment where their children can eat a snack, have some free time to move and run after sitting at a desk all day, and have time and space to work on homework. Based on these expectations, nine out of ten parents using after-school child care say that they are happy with their current arrangements (Afterschool Alliance, 2014).

After-school child care is used by all socioeconomic groups of families. The child-care subsidy program provided through the CCDBG provides funding for approximately 500,000 children per year to pay for before- and after-school child-care programs, as well as full-time summer programs for school-age children (Afterschool Alliance, 2020). In fact, children between six and thirteen years of age represent 34 percent of those receiving subsidy funding from the CCDBG funds (Afterschool Alliance, 2020). This level of enrollment shows that many low-income families need continued child care for their children to be able to maintain a job. It also shows that the school day is not long enough for working parents to have a safe place for their children, unless they receive additional support.

Since after-school programs typically provide transport for the children from the elementary schools to the child-care programs, the elementary school staff must collaborate with the after-school program to make sure that essential information is communicated to the families when needed. Also, the elementary schools must notify child-care programs when weather or emergencies demand that the schools close early, so that children can be picked up in a timely fashion. Families must work with both organizations to ensure smooth communication and to make sure that both the school and the child-care program know about days when the child will be absent or to ensure that the correct adults are listed on the emergency contacts and pick-up list.

The child-care programs may also reach out to the family resource centers at the elementary schools to make sure that the staff members know from which schools the centers pick up students, whether scholarships are available, and how the two programs can coordinate. It can be important for the child-care program to know what illnesses are spreading through the schools and on which days the school will be closed for holidays, in-service training for teachers, or poor weather. To make sure that children and families get quality care and needed support, communication is key.

When after-school child care is offered on-site at an elementary school, it can make many of these transitions much easier. Transportation is not needed to move children from the school day to after-school care. Children are already familiar with the school environment because they have been there all day. The elementary teachers are able to communicate more easily with the after-school caregivers on the same campus; however, it is still key that this communication occurs because parents are not able to speak directly with the classroom teachers when they pick their children up from after-school care each day.

An after-school program on-site at an elementary school typically has all the same days off as the public school does. This can be challenging for some families, since the public school system typically has twenty-nine days off during the school year, without weather emergencies, and the adults in the family may still need to go to work on those days. In those scenarios, the family will need to prepare for back-up child care.

PUBLIC PRESCHOOL

Preschool offered in a public school setting is typically state funded like the K–12 education system, and it is available to children who have a diagnosed disability and need special-education support and to students who are at risk for developmental delays due to low family incomes. Many states use the same income guidelines for their public preschool program that they use for free or reduced-cost lunch. Public preschool can be offered to children once they turn three years old, and they can use the services until they are eligible to start kindergarten. The main goal of state-funded preschool in most states is to assist low-income families and children with disabilities to be more prepared for kindergarten; however, five states offer universal preschool: Florida, Vermont, Oklahoma, Wisconsin, and West Virginia.

The public preschool standards are typically higher for both teachers and curriculum than the standards in privately funded preschool programs. Nationwide, the average cost of a year of public preschool is $13,655, which is about $1,000 more than the K–12 school system pays per child (Mongeau, 2018). This discrepancy is due to group sizes, educator qualifications, and special-education supports. The annual cost for public preschool for low-income families is far higher than the cost per child that most middle-income families can afford. Because the majority of middle-income families are not able to qualify for public preschool unless their children have a diagnosed disability, a discrepancy exists between the quality of care that low-income families can receive for free and that which middle-income families are able to receive based on their ability to pay.

Nationwide data shows that approximately 1.37 million children attend public preschool each year, making up almost one-third of those who attend public kindergarten (Mongeau, 2018). These children experience documented benefits through the public programs. Children who attend public preschool show higher rates of kindergarten success than those who attend other prekindergarten programs (Conger et al., 2019). More public preschool students are promoted to first grade on time, and they experience less school mobility from kindergarten to first grade (Conger et al., 2019). Also, English language learner (ELL) students are more likely to exit ELL services if they attended public preschool (Conger et al., 2019).

Public preschool teachers typically have a strong background in special-education supports, so they can help assess the students' development multiple times throughout the year and can focus on areas of development that need the most attention. Special-education therapists, such as speech and language pathologists, will come into the classroom to support students with their individual learning needs. Also, the school system already knows the educational expectations for kindergarten, so teachers will tailor the preschool curriculum to help prepare students for their kindergarten year of school.

Despite its many benefits, public preschool faces significant limitations. Many states offer only half-day preschool for three to four hours of care and education. This type of limited early education setting can be very challenging for working families to negotiate. If the adults in the home work for eight hours a day, they may not have a way to transfer the child from the public school to another early education setting. Some school systems will allow the school bus to transport a child from the public school to a child-care program, but an extended period on a school bus can be a challenge for many three- or four-year-old students. If the commute is not short, younger students may have an accident on the bus or fall asleep while waiting to arrive at the child-care program.

Because public preschool does provide special-education services to children with IEPs, many families do not want to miss out on that service and incur large medical bills when paying for these therapies on their own. This is one reason that many families enroll in public preschool and then pay for an additional child-care program for the rest of the school day. The family must usually pay the full cost of the other child-care program, even if the child attends for only a portion of the day. This is because the program forfeits the ability to enroll another child if it knows a student is arriving late each day. Some child-care programs have policies about children arriving late and missing the largest portion of learning time in the morning, so they may decline to enroll a child who would arrive each day after attending public preschool. It can be hard for a child to acclimate from one program to another, and the child-care program may not want to disrupt the learning of the other students. Despite the rationale, these inflexible policies can make child care very challenging for families who need to work a full day away from home.

PUBLIC-PRIVATE PARTNERSHIPS

Many public school systems and child-care programs—particularly those that use subsidy funding from the CCDBG—are attempting to find ways to work together to maximize funding and support working families. These partnerships can look very different, depending on the school system's approach. For example, in some public schools, the preschool classroom pursues a child-care license in order to participate in the state's quality rating system and receive the monetary awards for high-quality programs. Becoming a licensed child-care program can also allow low-income families to apply for a child-care subsidy. With the assistance of the subsidy dollars to fund additional staffing and expenses, programs that were previously open for three to four hours per day could expand to full-day care. Not only would children still get the benefit of a highly qualified public school teacher and special-education resources, but the families could also receive additional funding needed to supplement their incomes.

Another option for public preschool programs would be to add extended child care to the remainder of the day. The classroom would not need to be licensed, but the extended child-care program would need to obtain a license. The difference would be that the teachers would not have to maintain standards that are quite as rigid as those the public school system requires, but the subsidy funding would still be available to pay for staffing and consumables. Although many public schools have after-school child-care programs, most states do not allow licensed early childhood centers to combine with school-age care for long periods. The public school would have to make sure that the preschool students have a separate location for their extended care.

Both of these options would mean that the school would have to invest in classroom materials that they may not typically need, such as nap mats for preschool children to use each day to rest. However, these alternatives would allow some families who might typically turn down the program because of transportation challenges to attend. Of course, anytime a public school opens a program, expectations of community support, a strong relationship, and a communication system must be in place. If the public school could find a way to offer extended supports to its enrolled families (such as extended classroom care), then the school would not have to depend so much on outside businesses to offer their services.

Since both the child-care programs and the elementary schools may care for the same children year after year, they often develop strong bonds with the families and the children. It seems reasonable that both organizations can work together to help the families succeed.

Coordinating Services for Children with Special Needs

Another essential partnership between the public school and the child-care system is serving children with disabilities. Of course, parents and guardians must be involved in this process; they must waive confidentiality rights so that the school can share the IEPs and other critical information on their children. The school can play a huge supporting role in educating the child-care programs on how to work with these students to achieve necessary goals.

This is a critical partnership for public preschool students up through the age of thirteen who receive after-school or summer care from child-care programs. Children who have special needs thrive and learn best in natural environments where a child who does not have a special need would normally be: home, school, child care, summer programs, play groups, public parks, and so on. The school diagnostician or therapists may need to observe children with special needs in child care or in a summer program. The parent may ask a child-care provider to attend the admissions and release committee (ARC) meeting as an expert working with the child, to offer essential information. The child-care provider may need to reach out to the teacher or special-education teacher to make sure that the behavior management system used in child care aligns with the school's system. This collaboration can be a great asset for the child.

Collaboration between the child-care program and the mental-health team, the school nurse, or the family resource specialist can also serve the needs of the child. If the family is willing to have both the school-support teams and the child-care program collaborating, then both education programs should be willing to come together, outside the public school environment, for the sake of the child. Child-care programs do not typically have resources such as medical experts and mental-health specialists. When all the involved adults handle a child's health, behavior, and education with the same plan and desired goals, the child is much more likely to be successful.

Coordinating Meal Services

When a child is not at school due to scheduled days off, it can make it much harder for that child to receive proper nutrition. If that child attends a child-care program that provides meals, many of those nutritional concerns are resolved. However, if the child-care program does not serve meals and the family is responsible for providing the meals, it can be helpful for the school system and the child-care program to work together to make sure that no child misses out. Many schools will deliver meals to low-income families on days when the students do not come to school, especially if it is a long weekend. Some students may need those meals while attending a child-care program, or the family may prefer that the meal be dropped off at the child-care program to ensure that the family receives the food before the start of the weekend. Many child-care programs will have multiple children from the same school in their programs. They may also have a large proportion of students in their program who qualify for subsidies. Assisting with meal distribution can be another potential way for schools and child-care partners to continue their collaboration.

A LOOK AT A FAMILY RESOURCE CENTER

Aisha runs the family resource center for an elementary school that has approximately seven hundred children enrolled during a typical school year. She works with families to inform them about and help them coordinate the care their children need during the hours that the parents are working and to help them navigate their children's entry into elementary school.

Coordinating Care

School begins at 7:45 each morning, and it is out at 2:45 each afternoon. At the end of each school day, about 225 children have a parent, family member, or babysitter pick them up in the car line. A few older students walk home, since this neighborhood school is close to several subdivisions. Another large group of students ride buses to get home. The rest of the children need an alternative method of getting home at the end of the day. Many different off-site child-care programs have vans that pick students up at the school, and the school also runs an on-site after-school program. Approximately three hundred students use the school child-care program or ride to another child-care program each day. Based on the number of children who ride the bus home each day, there are probably many children that go home by themselves and are expected to stay home independently until a parent arrives from work.

From the start of school in the fall until the final day of school in the spring, the school system schedules approximately twenty-nine days off each year, including winter break and spring break. Aisha's school district approves those days before the previous school year is over so that each school can inform families of those dates well in advance. When parents are making plans for teacher in-service days and holidays, they rarely complain to the faculty and staff because they have time to find care for their children. Some parents do complain to the school over the cost of child care for a full day when the school is closed—the cost can be considerable—but if families have time to save the money, they are more likely to be able to handle the expense. Others occasionally remark that they have to use all of their paid time off for school holidays instead of saving time for a vacation. In general, though, most families understand the need for these small breaks from school.

When the school has an emergency closure, however, the parent response is very different. First, Aisha's school district does not usually cancel school for weather-related issues until 10 or 11 p.m. on the night before the day off; however, the district sometimes waits to announce a closure until 5 a.m. on the day of the cancellation. This gives parents very little time to plan. In addition, some child-care programs in the area follow the school calendar, so if the public school system is closed, the child-care program closes too. If low-income families are not at school due to weather, they also have to consider where the children will get their meals. Most child-care programs do remain open on snow days, but some staff members may not be able to drive in poor road conditions, so additional child care may not be available for students who do not regularly attend those programs. If the parent's employer is not flexible enough to let the employee work from home or bring the child into the office with her, the parent could potentially lose a full day of work. Of course, in Aisha's mind, the worse alternative is that the parent does go into work and leaves a second- or third-grade child at home alone.

When parents reach out to the family resource center to ask for contact information or recommendations about child-care programs in the area, Aisha is happy to help. She lets the families know which programs will pick children up at the school, and she can provide information about the on-site after-school care program. Many parents will tell her that the child-care programs in the area are just too expensive. She knows that child care is an enormous cost for families. She also can share information with them about the state subsidy programs that assist with child care, but most programs do not have any type of internal scholarship programs for families.

A public preschool program does operate at Aisha's school, but it is only three hours long. Children who qualify can attend a session from 7:30 to 10:30 a.m., or they can attend a session from 11:30 a.m. to 2:30 p.m. If children attend the morning session, child-care program vans will not come to pick them up in the middle of the day. If their parents cannot pick them up at 10:30 a.m., then the children will have to ride the school bus to their home or to a local child-care program. If the children attend the afternoon session, their parents will have to drop them off at the school, or they can ride a school bus from home or from their child-care center. Again, the child-care program vans do not drop off or pick up at school in the middle of the school day. Once the afternoon session of preschool is over, the children can be picked up by a parent or ride the school bus home, but they could also ride the child-care program van to a local child-care program. The school's on-site after-school care does not offer care for preschool students; it serves children only from kindergarten through fifth grade.

Some children in the school district have qualified for the public preschool but declined their spots because the families could not figure out the transportation piece of the puzzle. Aisha would try to assist the families with finding a local child-care program where the school bus would be able to pick up and drop off the children, but spots were not always available at the times the families needed them. Other families were very nervous about having their four-year-old child ride a school bus each day and just felt safer placing the child in full-day child care.

Navigating Kindergarten Entry

Before children enter kindergarten each year, families must make an appointment to come in and have one of the kindergarten teachers conduct developmental screening on their children. This screening does not prevent the children from attending kindergarten if they have a low score; the main objective is to help the school district get a sense of how many children are prepared to enter kindergarten. It also helps the teachers with the initial classroom placements so that children are evenly distributed into the different classrooms based on their needs and developmental abilities. The teachers typically ask the children to join them in the classroom so the children can show them a series of simple skills, such as telling the teacher their full names and drawing simple shapes with a pencil. While the parents wait for the children to complete the assessment, they fill out some necessary background information, including a question about whether or not the children have attended any type of child care or preschool before going to kindergarten. At Aisha's school, approximately 65 to 75 percent of the children entering kindergarten have previously attended some sort of child-care or preschool program.

Aside from the parent-survey information, it is typically very easy for the kindergarten teachers to determine which children have attended child care before entering kindergarten because their behavior is so different from the children who have not attended any type of child-care program. The kindergarten teachers' first clue is typically how easily the children separate from their parents at the screening or on the first day of school. The children who have attended child care also seem to follow group directions, adjust to changes in the schedule more easily, and develop friendships with their classmates more quickly than children who have stayed at home with a family member until entering school.

Appreciating the Work of Child-Care Programs

Aisha and her colleagues are typically very grateful for the child-care programs in the area because, when the children use child care after school or on snow days, they know that those children are not at home alone. Many of the child-care programs in the area have cared for the same children since they were very small, so the centers have strong relationships with the families. Aisha is also grateful that the child-care programs are there to support the families during holidays and summer vacations when the school system is not. One big concern for Aisha when the public school system is closed is that child abuse and domestic violence cases may not be reported when necessary and children could remain in dangerous living situations. Because child-care providers are mandatory reporters of abuse and domestic violence, many of these cases will not go unreported, even though the public school system is closed.

When the schools are open, child-care programs may reach out to Aisha with concerns about a child's behavior or with concerns that may be indications of abuse or neglect. Due to the Federal Education Rights and Privacy Act (FERPA), there is certain information that the school system is unable to share with a child-care program without parent or guardian consent. Regardless, Aisha can always document a call from a child-care provider and add the potential concerns to her data for IEP meetings or calls that she may need to make in the future to child and family services. The child-care programs may not have the exact requirements and methods as the public school system, but their overall goals are to take care of the children.

Child Care in the Time of COVID-19

When the pandemic began in Aisha's state, one of the first major closures was the public school system. The children would still be learning and attending school online, but no one would have daily, face-to-face contact with them. Since some of the children in the school district did not have computers or reliable internet service, the school system brainstormed ways to keep in contact with students. Many schools in Aisha's district simply distributed packets of worksheets for the children to complete and turn back in to the teachers. Aisha's school distributed laptops to all of the students who did not have computer access in their homes, so they could do assignments online each day. This made Aisha more comfortable than just distributing worksheet packets. If the children were logging on each day, then a teacher would see them and be able to ask them how they were doing. Young students might tell a teacher if they were not receiving enough food or if they were left alone for extended periods of time.

When the schools first closed to in-person classes, the child-care programs were still open, so child-care providers could still see many of the children from Aisha's school and make sure that they were okay. A week later, the state asked child-care programs to close except for serving children of essential employees, such as hospital staff, workers in the department of community-based services, and food-distribution employees. Consequently, the vast majority of children from Aisha's school were in their homes with no outside eyes on the families. Plus, the families were under more stress than they had experienced in years. Many parents had either lost their jobs or seen their hours cut back significantly. Many families who had not lost their jobs either had to work from home with the children in the house or had to resign their positions due to a lack of child care if they were not considered essential employees as defined by the state.

As weeks continued to pass, Aisha began to worry about what the children were experiencing without being in school or child care. For many children, a relative getting ill, a parent losing a job, or simply the dramatic change in routine had caused significant anxiety. Some children were so isolated that pediatricians were concerned about an increase in childhood depression. The school system was still offering meals at designated sites for families who qualified for free or reduced lunches, but not all the families who qualified for these meals were showing up as frequently as expected.

Aisha began to receive phone calls from families who had never needed support from the resource center before. Families who had lost a job were asking her how to get food from local food pantries and how to contact the government about unemployment and other benefits. Aisha created a resource guide for families to answer questions about how and where to get help. Some of Aisha's favorite resource-center programs, such as a birthday cake kit for children the week of their birthdays, were losing funding because all of the resource center's funds were being used to assist with major initiatives. Aisha sent an email out to all the teachers and parent-teacher association members asking whether anyone would be willing to sponsor birthday cake kits for fifteen dollars per student. She was amazed at all of the responses and donations that she received from the staff. They didn't want the students to miss out on celebrating their birthdays during this chaotic time.

The school year closed without Aisha and her coworkers getting to see the students again, but it appeared that child-care programs would be opening soon. Their reopening would enable more children to be around loving adults and would allow children to be in social environments that could help reduce their anxiety and loneliness. Once again, Aisha was extremely grateful for the child-care programs, especially those that provided two hot meals a day for families. Many families had experienced trauma that they were not ready to speak about with others yet. They may have lost a loved one, had to move to a smaller apartment, or lacked enough food for every family member during the course of the quarantine period. Returning to a normal routine in a child-care center with peers and loving caregivers would help many children reduce stress that had built up over the past few months.

Aisha worked over the summer to provide resources for the families in need at her school—a much larger number than in previous years. The end of the summer months brought increased cases in COVID-19, and once again the school system had to consider whether or not it was safe to have a building full of young children who could potentially spread the virus to one another and to their families. The school system eventually decided to begin the school year virtually to make sure that all teachers and children stayed as healthy and safe as possible; however, this time the child-care programs would remain open, but with slightly lowered capacity. Many families who had never used child care before were looking for a safe environment for their children during the day while the adults were at work. Child-care programs filled up quickly due to limited capacity and the number of elementary school students who now needed child care. Each day, Aisha continued to take calls from families who had questions about how to find child care for the first time since their children were very small. With each conversation, she hoped the family would be able to find safe care for their children.

These calls led her to believe that the alternative would be a parent forced to quit her job or a young child having to stay at home during the day while also trying to complete school work independently. This time, all schools in the district would be using online learning instead of worksheet packets. Teachers would get to see their students each day in virtual meetings and could ask the children if they were okay. If they were not, the school could send someone to check on the family. The children who were in child care each day would have someone at the child-care program checking on them and caring for them while supporting them with their school work. This was far from an ideal situation, but with the support of the virtual meetings and the child-care programs, at least the schools would know if more students were safe this time.

Chapter 9:
The Human-Services
Impact

Although a primary focus of child care is early education and school readiness, child-care programs also provide essential human services to keep children safe and to help make sure that their basic needs are met. Organizations such as the state department for children's services, the Child and Adult Care Food Program (CACFP), and Head Start can partner with child-care programs to benefit the children and their families. Some of these services may be for low-income families, but others serve families regardless of the family's socioeconomic status. Because families may be unaware that programs like these exist in the community, one key role of child-care programs is to help connect the families with these services.

MANDATORY REPORTING AND PREVENTING CHILD ABUSE

One important responsibility of all staff members who work in the child-care industry is to be mandatory reporters of child abuse. Although each state has different requirements about reporting suspected abuse, forty-seven states have laws on mandatory reporting of child abuse. The vast majority of those states include child-care providers as one of the professions that is legally required to report when they suspect that abuse is taking place (Children's Bureau, 2019). This does not mean that the child-care professional must wait until he has concrete proof of abuse. Most laws indicate that the mandatory reporter needs "reasonable cause" to report possible cases of physical, mental, or sexual abuse, or significant neglect (Children's Bureau, 2019).

The phrase *mandatory reporter* means that if the child-care provider suspects abuse and does not report that suspicion to the police or to the state's office of child and family services, the provider can face legal charges for withholding that information. Some child-care providers may report concerns to a coworker or an employer and expect that act to relieve them of the reporting requirement; however, if the coworker does not have direct knowledge of the potential abuse, then he or she is not able to make a report. Some employers will tell child-care providers that they must let them know before they make a report. It is fine for the staff member to collaborate with the employer; however, if a child-care professional suspects abuse, it is still that professional's responsibility to report regardless of what the employer says. Many states have a clause in their mandatory reporting laws that states that the employer cannot penalize the employee for reporting an event if he suspects abuse; that way a staff member never needs to worry about the possibility of losing her job for following the reporting laws (Children's Bureau, 2019).

Child-care providers who report potential child-abuse cases must also take into consideration the term *reasonable cause* (Children's Bureau, 2019). This means that with the information that has been observed, it is not unlikely that some type of abuse is happening. Child-care staff members who report abuse in order to seek revenge against a family or to benefit themselves in some way could experience negative repercussions. However, most states have a law in place to protect child-care providers who make a report in order to protect the children. These types of laws are often called "Good Samaritan Laws," based on the argument that the law is not meant to penalize someone who is trying to protect or help an individual in need.

Many child-care providers may be nervous to report a suspected case of child abuse, particularly if it is the first time that the staff member has ever done it. It is perfectly fine for a staff member to ask his supervisor to sit in on the call to help him through the process. It is also helpful if the child-care program has a template or worksheet that the staff member can fill out before the call, with all the necessary information so that the details are available if he gets nervous.

One important detail for child-care providers to remember is that they do not have to prove that abuse took place. That is the job of child and family services. The child-care provider just needs to alert the investigators that something looks suspicious, and the official agency will do the work to determine whether or not abuse took place. The investigators have the resources and the legal access to do a thorough investigation, so the child-care provider never needs to attempt to take on that role. The key role of the child-care provider is to care for the children in the classroom each day and to be the mandatory reporter if the need arises.

Despite their willingness to report, many child-care providers do not want to be identified as the individual who contacted child and family services. Many states have the option of anonymous reporting (Children's Bureau, 2019). If a child-care provider is worried about the family learning his identity, he can report anonymously. There are some disadvantages to anonymous reporting, however. It can be beneficial for child and family services to follow up with the person who made the report to ask additional questions; an anonymous report does not allow them to do that.

Due to the large number of hours that children spend in care with the child-care staff, family members may suspect that the report came from one of the teachers. Data shows that child-care providers in center-based care are much more likely to report potential child-abuse cases than providers who work in family child-care homes (McKenna, 2010). This trend could have several potential reasons. First, a child-care provider in a center-based program has a little more anonymity because many different adults work in the program. Even if a family suspects that a child-care staff member made the report, they still may not be able to determine which staff member did so. In a family child-care home, on the other hand, there is typically only one adult working with the children, so it is much harder to maintain anonymity. Second, some families may be offended if a staff member reports a potential abuse case to child and family services, and they may look for a different child-care setting after the investigation. In a child-care center, one family leaving the program will not have a significant financial impact, especially when the center staff members are comforted by knowing that they reported the potential abuse case in an effort to help the child. In a family child-care home, however, losing one family can have a much larger financial impact, so the provider may be more apprehensive about reporting. Despite the intimidating nature of filing a report of suspected child-abuse, regulated child-care programs, both center-based and home-based, have the potential to reduce child abuse significantly. The keys to reducing possible cases of abuse include program policies for staff members, parent education, and partnering with community organizations to help families as much as possible.

The American Academy of Pediatrics (AAP, 2018) states that most cases of child abuse come from within the child's family. This means that child-care providers are on the front lines to see both the risk factors for child abuse, as well as the signs that abuse is happening. Potential risk factors for abuse within the family include parental depression, a parent with a mental illness, a parent with a history of abuse in his own life, and domestic violence within the home (AAP, 2018). Of course, just because the family demonstrates risk factors does not mean that abuse is taking place. This is the perfect opportunity for child-care professionals to help prevent abuse cases by supporting the family and increasing communication between the family and the child-care program.

One early step for the child-care programs to take is to make sure that staff members are trained on identifying signs and symptoms of child abuse. It is also crucial that staff members know the process of how to report abuse. Child-care providers receive training on child abuse when they enter the field of child care, but for those who stay in the field for more than a few years, it can be very beneficial to have regular training on this topic. Most abuse happens to children who are age three and under, so it is even more important that infant and toddler caregivers have regular trainings on identifying child abuse and how to report it (McKenna, 2010). Centers can also help the process of reporting child abuse by making sure that the center's policies state that child-care providers will not be penalized for reporting potential abuse. This policy is even more effective when providers see the administration enforce the policy and help providers through the reporting process when they have questions.

Another way that child-care providers can assist in child-abuse prevention is by making parent education a priority in the classroom, especially for first-time parents. Parenting is stressful, and if parents lack a large toolkit of parenting skills, then they can stay frustrated a great deal of the time. Frustration can easily escalate when a parent is stressed and sleep deprived. Child-care providers are specialists in the field of working with children, so it is important to share their knowledge with parents. Some parents are not ashamed to ask questions. They will arrive every morning asking a teacher questions about feeding an infant or toilet-training a toddler. Other parents feel uncomfortable asking questions about their own children. To avoid singling out one family, a child-care provider can offer general education to the entire classroom or school. Some organizations, such as Zero to Three, have wonderful education flyers available on their website that child-care providers can distribute to families. Other providers may use a center-wide blog or a classroom newsletter to distribute information. It is essential for the parents understand that they are not alone and that there are resources available to help them.

It is also very important for parents to understand what their children are developmentally capable of achieving. If a parent of a one-year-old child tries to begin toilet-training, he will be much less successful than the parent of a slightly older child. Frustration can escalate, and a parent can become upset with the child and upset with himself. If the parent understands the child's developmental abilities, then he is much less likely to create unnecessary frustration. Child-care providers can also help parents seek help from a pediatrician or a developmental specialist when they notice that a child is not developing at a typical rate. Of course, child-care providers are not doctors or diagnosticians, so they never need to diagnose a condition for a young child; however, they have seen children fall behind developmentally and can alert the parent to concerns. Children who have special needs are more frequently abused than children who are developing at a typical rate. This can happen for a variety of reasons, such as a child constantly acting out or frustration that a child cannot complete typical skills. If a parent acknowledges the disability and gets additional support, then he is more likely to be able to handle the additional stress of the situation.

Child-care programs and schools have always been a key piece in identifying child abuse. During the spring of 2020, when very few children were reporting to child care or school in a face-to-face capacity, there was a significant decrease in reported cases of child abuse. This is an unusual finding, since many families were under additional financial and emotional stress accompanying the pandemic. For example, in Washington, DC, from mid-March through April, child abuse reports decreased by 62 percent, but the emergency room doctors did not see a decline in the types of injuries that typically result from abuse (CDC, 2020a). This leads to the realization that without child-care programs and schools reporting abuse, many abuse cases are occurring without anyone to report those cases and pursue help for those children. Child-care providers have a significant role in keeping young children safe, and without access to safe child care during the day, those numbers could continue to increase.

CHILD SAFETY AND HEALTH

The state and federal requirements for regulated child-care programs help make child-care programs safe places for young children. For example, all employees in regulated child care must have background checks. These checks, conducted both in center-based child care and in family child-care homes, are an effort to make sure that the staff members have not been charged with child abuse or neglect in the past and that they are not on a sex offenders' registry. Background checks also look for other serious crimes that would keep the candidate from being a good choice to work with young children. In family child-care homes, additional background checks are conducted on the other family members who live in the home because they may also interact with the children.

A regulated child-care center must set up a safe and healthy environment where the children can stay engaged in developmentally appropriate activities. These programs are inspected by the state to make sure that they remain healthy and safe, to reduce the spread of illness and the risk of injury. When children are enjoying activities meant for their age and developmental level, they are less likely to be injured by playing unsafe games. Center-based child care and some family child-care homes also have the added benefit of multiple adults being with the same group of children, which creates increased accountability.

THE CHILD AND ADULT CARE FOOD PROGRAM

The Child and Adult Care Food Program (CACFP) is a federal program that can reimburse child-care centers and family child-care homes for the meals and snacks that they serve to eligible children if they meet the established criteria for nutritious meals (US Department of Agriculture [USDA], 2019). The CACFP is typically administered through a state agency that partners with child-care programs. The state agency can offer cash reimbursements to the child-care programs that provide documentation that they served meals and snacks that meet the federal food-program guidelines to eligible children. The child-care programs can be reimbursed for up to two meals and one snack per day for each eligible child. If the child-care program serves a food that does not meet the guidelines, the state agency will not reimburse the program for that particular food.

Child-care centers are reimbursed at different rates depending on whether or not the children in their programs qualify for assistance. Children can be classified as eligible for free meals, reduced-price meals, or paid meals. The reimbursement payment is then calculated based on the cost of the food provided and the number of children who attended the program. In family child-care homes, all meals are served free; however, if the child-care provider's home is in a low-income neighborhood, the reimbursement rate is higher.

Child-care providers that participate in the CACFP can offer the children they care for several benefits that may not be available to other child-care programs. First, by providing healthy, balanced meals to children starting at a young age, providers can help children with brain development and physical growth at a crucial time in their lives. Of course, families know that these nutritious meals are important for young children, but with busy family lifestyles, they may not always have the opportunity to prepare healthy meals for their children at home. The CACFP offers children and families the assurance that children are receiving these healthy food choices throughout the day. Second, children begin forming healthy eating habits from a young age, so being introduced to a variety of fruits and vegetables supports lifelong practices. Children are able to establish a pattern of being curious about new foods and willing to taste items they may not have eaten before at home.

Third, children who eat healthy meals each day are less likely to be sick or to experience fatigue (AAP, 2020b). A healthy diet helps children develop strong immune systems, improves mood and memory, strengthens bones and teeth, and can even improve sleep patterns. A specialist from CACFP can visit the center to offer education to children about why healthy foods are good for them, further supporting their healthy eating habits. Many children many not be receiving high-quality food, or enough food, at home, so child-care programs that offer this type of nutrition to the children they serve are improving the children's overall quality of life.

The CACFP is offered only to regulated child-care programs, so it can be an incentive for programs (particularly unregulated family child-care homes) to seek regulation so that they can receive this reimbursement. Even if a child-care provider is not following the guidelines of the federal food program, food can still be a large expense. If the provider participates in the program and buys the healthier foods, the reimbursement will still lower the provider's food costs compared to previous costs. Some programs, such as Head Start, require their child-care programs to participate in the CACFP. Some states have minimum regulatory requirements that are so close to the CACFP guidelines that very few changes are needed for a program to participate and receive the reimbursement.

WORKING IN THE FIELD

Miriam works in a rural state in the Southeast, where there is a large amount of poverty. She works for the state agency that partners with child-care programs for the CACFP, currently partnering with just over one thousand child-care programs that feed more than forty-five thousand children daily throughout the state. These child-care programs include regulated child-care centers, regulated family child-care homes, and licensed Head Start programs. Miriam's primary job is to train the child-care program directors on what types of food they can serve at their programs in order to be reimbursed. She also trains center directors on how to fill out the CACFP paperwork and how to document their spending so they can be reimbursed for the largest possible amount of food. She also offers tips such as creating a cycle menu, so that the programs don't have to come up with new menus every month.

Although all child-care programs in the state could benefit in some ways from participating in the CACFP, Miriam works with the programs that initiate a partnership. The programs must be willing to change both their menus and their billing processes to participate in this type of program. She has found that when a program partners with the CACFP only reluctantly, that program usually drops out due to their unwillingness to meet the requirements. Miriam and her colleagues have become accustomed to sharing essential information with child-care providers to explain the benefits of the program and then letting the providers decide whether they want to participate.

Sometimes Miriam is shocked that the providers' greatest challenge is their own lack of understanding of what healthy meals look like. Miriam offers some education to the providers, but she also offers sample menus that the programs can start off using until they are more comfortable with the meal-planning components. The meal plans focus on milk, protein, grain, vegetables, and fruit, but the providers also have to consider added sugar and appropriate serving sizes. Many providers get confused when Miriam discusses vegetarian options for protein, as well as what whole-grain options look like. All of this initial training is an investment in the child-care providers' success.

Training child-care providers on the CACFP paperwork also takes a lot of time. Some programs, such as Head Start, will work with an agency or main office to get support from the nutrition manager with their paperwork. Other programs are independent organizations, and the paperwork may be the most difficult piece for them. If the child-care program has a billing expert who handles tuition and payroll, Miriam will often work with that specialist on how to complete the CACFP paperwork. However, most child-care programs have a single director who must handle all the administrative work.

Miriam can train the program director to order food using the menu to meet the CACFP guidelines. The program must meet the minimum serving requirements for each child to be reimbursed, and most directors want to have extra for children who need seconds, especially if they do not receive enough food at home.

During Miriam's time working with the CACFP, she has seen some centers stay with the program and others come and go. When she sees a program drop out of the CACFP, one of her biggest concerns is whether the children are getting enough food to eat. The CACFP sets minimum serving sizes for many of the foods that providers serve to children, and when programs start participating in the program, Miriam notices that many of them are trying to reduce the serving size in order to save money.

Serving sizes are typically done by age range and by type of food. For example, when directors order milk, they will need to look at the numbers of toddlers, preschoolers, and school-age children. Based on those totals, they will use the required serving sizes for the minimum amount of milk to order. The same process will happen for all the items on the first week of the menu. This is another reason that Miriam recommends a cycle menu. A center that uses a three-week cycle will find it easier to determine the amounts of each food that should be ordered each week.

It is essential that the child-care programs offer enough healthy food to make sure that children do not suffer from malnutrition. That is one of the driving reasons that Miriam has worked with the federal food program for so long. When she offers training in the centers and family child-care homes, she sees the students who desperately need the food program to meet their basic needs. She knows that children who come to child care hungry each day are not thinking about learning their shapes or numbers; they are thinking about when they get to eat. Helping the child-care programs serve healthy meals meets some of the students' basic needs, and then they have the ability to focus on learning.

THE BENEFITS OF HEAD START

After President Lyndon B. Johnson launched his War on Poverty in 1964, Sargent Shriver, director of the Peace Corps and special assistant to the president, met with a panel of experts to create a child-development program that would benefit the most vulnerable children (Office of Head Start, 2019). The Head Start program was launched in 1965, serving 560,000 preschool students living in poverty.

Since the beginning of the program, it has continued to evolve to serve children who are most in need of early education and care so they can be successful when they start elementary school. In 1980, Head Start began an inclusive approach to assist children with disabilities to prepare for starting elementary school. In 1995, the Early Head Start program was created to serve children from birth to the age of three years. In 1997, the Head Start program began to create partnerships with child-care programs in an effort to maximize the distribution of Head Start services to children who were already enrolled in child care. In 2014, Early Head Start partnerships began to serve the infant and toddler population that was already enrolled in full-time child care but still qualified and needed Early Head Start's variety of support services (Office of Head Start, 2019).

Head Start offers not only part-day and full-day child care and education but also a variety of other services for the children and their families. Children enrolled in Head Start or Early Head Start programs have access to developmental screenings, healthy meals through the CACFP, immunizations, dental and vision screenings, and medical visits (Office of Head Start, 2019). Families who participate in the Head Start system have access to stable housing, GED programs and other continued education, and programs for financial education and stability (Office of Head Start, 2019). Head Start strives to support the whole family by not only offering parent and child events, but also by offering parent-education classes that can help reduce stress and potential abuse by helping parents understand child development.

Head Start programs specifically focus on families who are in the most need. Families qualify for Head Start services if the total family income is at or below the FPL. Families also qualify if they are homeless or if the family already receives TANF or supplemental security income (Office of Head Start, 2019). Children who are in foster care qualify for Head Start regardless of the family's economic status, and up to 10 percent of a Head Start program's enrollment slots can go to children with disabilities, even if the families are outside the income guidelines (Office of Head Start, 2019).

Funding for Head Start and Early Head Start is provided by the federal government, but it is not issued to a lead agency at the state level. Private organizations throughout the state write grant proposals requesting funds from the federal government, based on the number of Head Start and Early Head Start children they anticipate serving (Office of Head Start, 2019). Those dollars are issued through a multiyear contract, and the organization will have to rewrite the grant application to continue the funding when the contract expires.

There are separate grants for Head Start programs and Head Start/Child Care Partnership arrangements. In a partnership grant, the Head Start grantee will partner with local child-care providers that already serve children in poverty. The child-care program will find a group of children who qualify for Head Start, and then those children can receive Head Start services even though they attend the child-care program. To enter the partnership, the child-care program must meet the requirements of a Head Start program, such as teacher education, child-to-staff ratios, developmental assessments, and curriculum. In turn, the Head Start program will provide additional services for those children and their families.

Head Start and Early Head Start partnerships with child-care programs challenge the child-care directors to improve the health, safety, and learning standards throughout the entire program so that families do not ask why certain classrooms have higher standards. Most child-care programs cannot offer the medical care and other health services that Head Start does; however, the child-care program can potentially increase teacher-education levels or lower classroom ratios throughout the building to mirror the Head Start requirements. Many Head Start programs are only half-day programs, but the Head Start partnerships can allow children to receive full-day services with a combination of Head Start funding and state subsidy dollars, so that children are in a safe and healthy environment all day while the parents or caregivers are at work. This practice of blending funds from different sources can allow children to experience the benefits of both programs.

The Head Start collaboration with child care allows children to experience a lot of services that child-care providers would not typically have the funding to pay. For example, Head Start programs have nutrition, mental-health, and disability specialists on their staff. Those specialists would come to the partnership site only to assist the child-care providers with a Head Start child; however, the training that the provider receives from the specialists can assist with other children in the classroom. Also, once a specialist is in the classroom, it is easy for the child-care provider to ask simple questions about room arrangement, behavior management, and positive reinforcement that can help several children who have disabilities. Head Start–partnership teachers also get access to a wide variety of training to which typical child-care programs may not be able to access. Head Start will train the child-care providers on setting individualized goals within the lesson plans, using classroom assessment, conducting observation and documentation, and implementing research-based practices. These trainings can have a very positive effect on the child-care program staff and the children they serve.

The Head Start system sees many families in the most vulnerable situations. These educators use their observations of the family to provide the best possible resources and to help the children and the families thrive. By assigning a case worker for each family, doing home visits, and sending frequent communication, Head Start and Early Head Start staff members learn a lot about the families with whom they work each year. Their staff may be some of the first people close to the family to detect abuse, domestic violence, or substance abuse. They can see the family's living situation and help them to find more stable housing. They can identify that a child is not developing at a typical pace and assist the family with getting assistance quickly to prevent any further problems. One of the downfalls of the Head Start system is that it serves so few children in comparison to the number of children who could benefit from this type of extensive service. These services are critical, and they need to be offered to more families in order to give more children the opportunity to leave poverty behind and be successful in the future.

SERVING VULNERABLE FAMILIES

Erika is the director of a rural Head Start program that serves approximately 270 children at any one time. She has been in this position for eight years, and her organization has supported a lot of families during that time. The slots in Erika's grants include Head Start and Early Head Start as well as partnership slots. Head Start slots are available in multiple communities, but there are fewer Early Head Start slots, particularly because they cost much more to support. Erika's organization includes the Head Start and Early Head Start classes, as well as family-service workers who support the families and make sure that the basic needs of the children are met. They also assist with recruitment each year by going out into the low-income communities to find families who qualify for the program and explain why Head Start and Early Head Start would benefit them.

When a family enrolls in a Head Start program, Erika's staff receives a thorough history on the family so that they know how to support them. The family-service staff makes sure that the families have medical and dental appointments, housing, heating and cooling, food, clothing, and internet access. They also make sure that the children have everything they need for school, including diapers, formula, clothing, meals, and snacks. They also make sure that the parents have access to workforce training and education, and they inform the family of events they may want to participate in.

Erika's Head Start programs collaborate with the public school system to make sure that children with developmental delays get an IEP and that the necessary special-education teachers and therapists come to the Head Start program each week to work with the children. Erika also makes sure that the classroom staff have the training that they need to work with children who exhibit challenging behaviors. Early Head Start and Head Start programs do not suspend or expel students. They continue to work with them regardless of complicated behaviors, so it is essential that teachers receive all the assistance they need to help the children. This also means that Erika has at least one disability specialist in her central office to help the teachers when needed and to assess the behaviors in the classroom and offer suggestions on how to guide children's behavior.

Many of the parents who have children in Erika's program had very negative experiences when they were students in school, so it is essential for the teachers to show them that their children are in an encouraging and happy classroom setting. Special-education meetings to review an IEP can also be difficult for many of the parents who also received special education when they were in school. Erika's staff members do everything they can to support the families through this process. They can provide transportation to the school and stay with the family during the meeting. They can make sure that the entire focus of the conversation is not about what the child cannot do but that it also focuses on the child's strengths and growth over the past year. They also try to make sure that the family has a positive introduction to the special-education teacher, the speech pathologist, and any other specialists the parent might not see on a daily basis, given that services are provided in the classroom setting.

Erika does not want parents to come to the classrooms only for drop-off, pickup, and serious meetings. She works hard to establish a family atmosphere in her programs, so her teachers and family-service workers collaborate to arrange monthly events at which the families feel welcome and have a good time at the school. This can be a new feeling for parents who grew up dreading going to school each day. The Head Start program also offers a variety of parent-education programs. In the past year, Erika and her team have led parent-education nights on picking the correct car seat, co-parenting with blended families, how to read a child's IEP, what types of questions to ask at a pediatrician visit, and what to expect if your child suffers from anxiety.

Erika's team also has twenty slots for children in Migrant Head Start. The schedule for Migrant Head Start is different from a typical school calendar. This program is for families who typically move into the area in March or April to do farming work and stay through the end of a harvest season. Since agriculture is a major part of the economy in Erika's state, her staff usually finds plenty of families who need to utilize the Migrant Head Start program. Many of the children and families in the program do not speak English as their primary language, so it is important to have several staff members who are bilingual and can speak to the families and make sure that they are receiving accurate communication from the program.

In the past several years, Erika's program has grown the number of partnership slots available for Head Start and Early Head Start. These partnerships have been more challenging than working with her own employees. As the director of Head Start for her program, she can easily enforce the Head Start guidelines that her employees will follow, and employees who do not want to follow those guidelines do not have to continue to work for her agency. The child-care partnership programs must be approached in a different way. Although these programs receive funding from Erika's Head Start program, they have different management and are owned and directed by individuals who do not report to Erika. It is essential to encourage these programs to rise to the same level as the Head Start standards, and the best way to do that is to convince the child-care programs that doing so will benefit the children, their teachers, their enrollment, and their bottom line.

Erika sends compliance officers to the child-care programs each week to monitor whether they are meeting the requirements of a Head Start partnership. At times, Erika feels that the child-care programs comply only when her staff members are on-site at the centers and holding them accountable. Of course, some centers are more compliant than others. Erika's Head Start program is able to pay more than most of the independent child-care programs in her area, so she is able to hire more qualified staff members than most of the child-care partnership sites. The Head Start policies and procedures require a great deal of work from the teachers, and it is hard to keep staff motivated to do that immense work load if they are making only minimum wage.

Low salaries at the centers also lead to high turnover, so Erika's leadership team frequently has to train new staff at the child-care partnership sites on what is required of Head Start teachers. When the centers are low on staffing, the compliance officers will often report that the adult-to-child ratios are higher than Head Start and Early Head Start will allow, but the centers have no more available staff members to place in the classrooms. Staff morale becomes low when the child-care program staff members have to work extended hours. Then turnover will spike again.

The concepts being implemented in the Head Start and Early Head Start partnership programs are beneficial for students and the programs, but it still seems insurmountable for the setup to work at some centers. Staffing, teacher education, and center policies can make it challenging for the center directors, even when they strive to follow all of the Head Start requirements listed in their contracts. Head Start funding is a huge resource to the child-care programs, but sometimes it is just assisting them with paying their basic bills before the lowered ratios go into place. If they can barely pay their bills with high ratios, what will happen when ratios are lowered? The system is set up to support the children and families, but changes need to be made in the child-care programs to help them meet and maintain the higher Head Start principles.

Chapter 10:
Children with Special
Needs in Child Care

Finding child care can be difficult for many families, but finding child care for a child with special needs is a huge challenge. *Special needs* can include diagnosed disabilities, sensory impairment, medical conditions, and mental-health disorders. Children living in foster care and children who have experienced trauma also have special needs. All of these children need additional supports to be successful in a classroom setting, and parents must find a child-care program that offers these extra supports.

Currently more than 1.7 million children in the United States under the age of six have at least one specialized health condition that requires continuous treatment (CCA, 2019). Another 5.7 million children in the United States under the age of six have at least one special need that challenges their ability to function in a typical classroom setting (CCA, 2019). This means that a typical child-care program may not meet the needs of these children. For children who are typically developing, 25 percent of their parents have a difficult time finding qualify child care (Mader, 2020). Research shows that 34 percent of parents of children with special needs struggle to find child care (Mader, 2020).

Many parents of children with special needs cannot find consistent child care due to the children's additional needs. Parents must attempt to set up complicated networks of care in which family members and friends volunteer to watch the children on different days and times. This type of care can be upsetting for this population of children because many of them need a consistent schedule with a trained caregiver. Parents of children with special needs are twice as likely as parents of typically developing or abled children to leave a job, not take a job, or make a significant job change due to lack of child care (Mader, 2020). This shows that not only do the children need additional support, but the families as a whole also need more support from the child-care community.

BARRIERS FOR THE FAMILY

As detailed in chapter 6, searching for child care already has its fair share of barriers. Parents must find a center that they can afford. If they don't have the money to pay for tuition, then it is pointless to pursue learning more about the program. The location and hours of operation are also key factors. The center has to be open during the times the parent is required to be at work, with enough leeway for the commute to and from the center. If the center is so far away from the family's home or from the parent's employer that she cannot get to the center in time for drop-off and pick-up, then the care does not meet the family's needs. Health and safety are extremely important for child-care programs. A parent must know that the child is safe at the child-care program in order to feel comfortable leaving the child there each day. If the parent doubts the child's safety in any way, the child will not remain enrolled in the program for very long, and the parent must start the search for child care all over again.

After searching for the foundational basics, parents also hope to find child-care providers who are warm and nurturing with their children. They seek programs with structured schedules that implement quality curricula. They want to find diverse programs where children have the opportunity to interact with children from a variety of backgrounds. Parents are also searching for child-care programs that involve the families in the children's learning through strong communication and family events. These standards are challenging to find in programs that are affordable for most families. The parent of a child with special needs must add an additional list of qualifications to the care she is looking for.

Parents of a child with special needs want to find child-care providers who have experience working with their child's particular needs. They want a program with low staff-to-child ratios so the child-care providers will be able to give their child enough attention so she can participate in the same activities as the other children. Parents need to make sure that the facility's building is accessible for their child and that their child's occupational therapist is welcomed into the building at least once a week to help support their child in a natural environment. They need the assurance that the teachers are not uncomfortable or nervous about interacting with their child in the classroom.

Child care is a high-turnover field. If a child-care provider is working with a child who has significant special needs or behavior challenges, it is especially important that the same teacher is there every day to support that child and establish consistency. Child-care programs are independent businesses, and they can establish parent and staff policies in the way they choose. Those policies, such as a rule that a child cannot move to a preschool classroom until she can use the restroom independently, must not unintentionally discriminate against children with disabilities.

In the event that parents do find a program that meets all of these needs, there is often a significant waiting list. Some programs have such a long waiting list that a child could completely age out of child care before moving to the top of the list of candidates. This type of waiting list suggests a great demand for specialized care; however, once many parents are offered a spot, they still may not be in a position to accept. The true cost per child for this type of child care is often much more than a family can pay. The Americans with Disabilities Act (ADA) prevents a child-care program from charging more for one particular child than the other children receiving the same services. Instead of charging a high rate of tuition for the child with special needs, the additional costs must be distributed to all children in the program. This means that many families would not be able to afford the cost of care, and the program would not generate enough income to stay in operation.

So, can't a child with special needs simply attend a public preschool? The Individuals with Disabilities Education Act (IDEA), Part B, outlines services for preschool children with disabilities, and these services are typically carried out in public preschool settings. This means that a preschool child with disabilities could enroll in public preschool and find a teacher with special-education training and therapists, such as speech pathologists, occupational therapists, and behavior analysts, who are trained to support the child's individual education needs. However, the barrier for many children to attend public preschool is that many states offer only half-day preschool. This means that working parents still need to find a safe location for their child for the remainder of the school day. It could also mean that a parent may have to travel to the school and transport the child to child care in the middle of the workday. For many families, this type of care arrangement is just not possible.

The IDEA, Part C, outlines services for infants and toddlers with special needs to get the special education services they need; however, once again, this approach does not connect with full-day child care. The typical state model allows for the special-education specialist to visit the child in her natural environment to provide therapy on a regular basis, depending on the child's needs. This could mean that the therapist visits the child at home to provide services or that the specialist visits the child in the child-care setting, since that is also a natural environment for a child who attends full-time child care. This type of arrangement can be beneficial for the child-care provider, because she can watch the therapist work with the child or participate in the therapy, when possible, to learn how to support the child when the therapist is not present. Despite the coaching that the specialist can offer the child-care provider, it still does not equal full-time inclusive child care. Furthermore, if the child-care provider participates in the therapy instead of the family, then the family misses out on the education. The IDEA does offer amazing services, but many supports are still needed for the birth-to-five-year-old population.

BARRIERS FOR THE CHILD-CARE PROVIDERS

Cost

Not only is it challenging for parents to find child care for children with special needs, it is also challenging and costly for child-care programs to provide that type of specialized care. Based simply on lower staff-to-child ratios, so that each child can receive more individualized education, child-care programs must take in less income but provide more in-depth services. Low ratios are best practice for child-care programs, regardless of the children that they serve, but care providers can lower the ratios only to a point. Too low, and they will not be able to cover the cost. Again, this means that tuition is often increased so that necessary expenses are still covered, even though fewer children are in attendance. High-quality programs, such as Head Start and Head Start partnerships, have already established lower ratios than many states require. In private-pay child-care settings, however, lowering the ratios and increasing the costs means that only affluent families can afford to attend these programs. Even families who receive a child-care subsidy would likely have to pay an overage fee that many low-income families cannot afford.

Child-care programs may also struggle with the cost of making their program ADA compliant (Henley and Adams, 2018). This typically means making physical alterations to the building, so that individuals with disabilities can have full access to the entire facility. For a child-care program, the typical building alterations could include ramps in and out of the building, a playground with surfaces that easily allow a child who uses a wheelchair or walker to use the playground equipment, and classroom tables that allow a child in a wheelchair to roll up to participate in activities. These types of alterations, especially the playground equipment, can be extremely costly. If the program has had little or no demand for these type of adaptations, it may not see the need for investing in the cost of the alterations.

Inconsistent Demand

Another factor influencing the availability of child care for children with special needs is the unreliable demand for this type of care (Henley and Adams, 2018). If parents do not anticipate that they will be able to find and afford specialized center-based child care for their children with special needs, they may go ahead and make long-term plans for their children's care outside of the child-care system. If the families in an area rely on a nanny or a nanny-share, then when center-based care does have an available slot, it may no longer be in demand. This does not mean that their individualized care is better than a high-quality center. Some children with significant needs may need individualized care in their own homes, but many children with special needs can benefit from an inclusive classroom setting with daily social opportunities and positive peer role models. The families have simply given up hope that this classroom setting exists or that there will be available openings, so they no longer pursue them.

Training

Another barrier to providing quality care for children with special needs is training staff members (Henley and Adams, 2018). Every state has educational requirements for its child-care teachers and caregivers; however, many educators take a position in child care without training or a degree that is focused on working with young children. Even those who pursue a child development associate (CDA) degree or a college degree in child development typically have minimal course work on special education. They may take a general course with an overview of the special-education system and an introduction to many common disabilities, but this general knowledge will not prepare a teacher to work with a full classroom of students, including several with special needs.

Many child-care providers do not feel confident or comfortable working with children with special needs (Henley and Adams, 2018). Because they have worked in programs that usually serve typically developing children, they are often cautious when they must make changes to their teaching strategies or their classroom environments. These are providers who dedicate their whole day to serving young children, and they must make individual adaptations for every child in the classroom, even children without special needs. They have the skill set to make these adaptations, but they may have been told by families and the community that they are not professionals. After hearing that message for years, it is understandable that they would doubt their abilities. Many teachers can easily support children with diverse needs simply by getting to know them and following guidance from the families, but they must have the confidence to do so.

Child-care educators need continuous training on disabilities and challenging behaviors. A two-hour professional development training on autism or childhood anxiety will not give a teacher the skills necessary to support a child with special needs. Of course, child-care providers still need these training hours on special education, but they also need coaching and mentoring in the classroom setting. A child's speech pathologist or occupational therapist who offers therapy in the classroom setting offers a good opportunity for developing the child-care provider's skill set, but more coaching and mentoring is needed. The local Child Care Resource and Referral (CCR and R) network needs to provide classroom observation and feedback on room arrangement, behavior management, and positive redirection that can help the child-care provider develop a skill set that can benefit her in the classroom for years to come.

Staff Turnover

Another factor that plays into training staff members on supporting children with special needs is the turnover rate in child-care programs. If a program director invests hours and funding into in-depth training for a child-care provider to work with children who have special needs, the director needs that provider to stay at the center. If the child-care provider leaves soon after the training is complete, the director must begin the training and coaching process all over again. When directors have frequent turnover in their programs, they will often stop in-depth training because they are simply losing money. The best way to break the turnover cycle is to pay child-care providers a salary that will discourage them from leaving. Of course, this means that a director must either charge the parents higher tuition or find an outside funding source that subsidizes the increased cost of care.

SUSPENSION AND EXPULSION

More than fifty thousand preschool students are suspended from preschool each year (Gorsky, 2018). Preschool expulsion is three times more likely to occur than expulsion from a K-12 program (Head Start ECLKC, 2020). Of those children who are expelled, preschool boys are four times more likely to be expelled than girls, and African American children are twice as likely to be expelled as children from Latino or white families (Head Start ECLKC, 2020). In Chicago, data showed that 42 percent of child-care programs that serve children from birth to age three have expelled at least one child during the previous year, and in Philadelphia, at least 26 percent of programs had expelled at least one child in the previous year (Gorsky, 2018). These studies also show that expulsion of a toddler is just as common as that of a preschooler. Toddlers are most frequently expelled due to frequent biting and an inability to be completely toilet-trained before moving to the preschool classroom.

Some child-care programs do not officially expel a child, but they utilize a technique known as "soft expulsion" (Gorsky, 2018). Soft expulsion occurs when the center pressures the parents into withdrawing the child on their own. The center may continuously call the family to ask them to pick the child up for the rest of the day because they have reached the maximum number of times a child can bite without being sent home. These types of strategies make it challenging for families to work a full day without interruption, and they eventually must find alternative care to protect their jobs.

Policy analysts Cristina Novoa and Rasheed Malik (2018) write that 12 percent of the children enrolled in child care have a disability, yet children with disabilities account for 75 percent of the children who are suspended or expelled from child care. Their numbers are based on data from the 2016 National Survey of Children's Health, conducted by the US Census Bureau. Novoa and Malik find that children with disabilities are 14.5 times more likely to be expelled or suspended than children who are typically developing. Research has also shown that children who have experienced more adverse childhood experiences (ACEs) are more likely to demonstrate challenging behaviors and be expelled from child care (Novoa and Malik, 2018).

Based on these numbers, it is obvious that teachers need more training, especially on social and emotional development. Academic curriculum development has been a focus in preschool for the past five to ten years, but training on social and emotional skills has not been the top priority for the early childhood field until recently. In fact, in 2012 only 20 percent of early childhood professionals received training on children's social and emotional needs (Novoa and Malik, 2018). Now, the increase of challenging behaviors indicates that social and emotional development should still be at the heart of early childhood education.

Most expulsions can be linked to challenging behaviors (Head Start ECLKC, 2020). Although child-care providers expect all classrooms to have some amount of challenging behaviors, the accumulation of these behaviors can have a dramatic impact. If a teacher becomes overwhelmed with the amount of challenging behaviors in the classroom, the program management is at risk of losing the staff member or losing the families whose children are demonstrating the significant behaviors. If the teacher is a true asset to the program, the program may choose to ask the family to leave.

Teachers may be unable to cope for different reasons. Those who are newer to the field may be overwhelmed by challenging behaviors due to lack of education or experience (Head Start ECLKC, 2020). They can also become overwhelmed by high adult-to-child ratios and large workloads. Another stressor for many teachers is that they misunderstand the reasons for the challenging behaviors (Head Start ECLKC, 2020). An inexperienced teacher may see a child continuously demonstrating inappropriate behaviors and associate the behavior with disobedience instead of trauma, anxiety, or an undiagnosed disability. When these overwhelming behaviors do surface, child-care programs often do not have the resources to support the children, and then the teachers are pushed to an extreme stress level.

Being expelled from preschool causes long-term side effects both for the child and for the family. Children who are expelled from an early education program are more likely to develop ongoing behavior problems (Head Start ECLKC, 2020). There are long-term effects to their development, their education, and their health. Many children develop low self-esteem after being removed from a child-care program (Head Start ECLKC, 2020). At a young age, they assume that they are not capable of learning and begin to give up. These same children also develop negative views about school and about teachers (Head Start ECLKC, 2020). When researchers look at long-term outcomes for children expelled from preschool, they also find significant correlations to truancy, dropping out of school, and incarceration (Novoa and Malik, 2018).

The families of the young children who are expelled also experience negative side effects. One of the most common is a significant increase in stress (Head Start ECLKC, 2020). When a family does not have secure child care, many other areas of family life are affected. The top priority becomes looking for alternative child care, but it can be challenging to find care under the best of circumstances, not to mention when a child is demonstrating difficult behaviors. Without consistent child care, it is easy for a parent to lose a job or be demoted for inconsistent attendance. The financial impacts can place a great deal of stress on the family.

The family can also experience social and emotional side effects when their child is expelled (Head Start ECLKC, 2020). It can be very easy for a parent to begin to blame the child or herself for letting the situation escalate to expulsion. Of course, a parent is not at the child-care program during the day, so she cannot control the behavior of the child; however, many parents will still feel a sense of responsibility for the situation. If the parent blames the child for the expulsion, then that can put an enormous strain on the relationship. In cases where the parent is angry at the child, the parent may even develop harsh parenting behaviors or abusive disciplinary tactics (Head Start ECLKC, 2020).

Although the presence of a disability can make a child demonstrate more challenging behaviors, not all disabilities have this side effect. A child with a fine-motor delay, for example, may be very successful in the classroom until she must hold a crayon or a pair of scissors. A child with a speech-articulation disorder may have a difficult time producing blended consonant sounds, but that delay would not necessarily lead to inappropriate classroom behavior. Several types of delays can cause much more friction in the classroom on a daily basis:

- Children with behavior problems are 43 times more likely to be expelled.

- Children with attention-deficit hyperactivity disorder (ADHD) are 33 times more likely to be expelled.

- Children with anxiety are 14 times more likely to be expelled.

- Children with autism spectrum disorder are 10 times more likely to be expelled.

- Children with a developmental delay are 7.5 times more likely to be expelled.

- Children with a speech disorder are 4 times more likely to be expelled (Novoa and Malik, 2018).

Some of these disorders may not seem to correlate with their statistics. It is essential for child-care providers to understand the root nature of a child's behavior. For example, how would a child with anxiety show challenging behaviors that would cause her to be expelled from preschool? The source of the behaviors for a child with anxiety is stress or worry; however, it does not always present as a child crying because she is afraid. Many children with high levels of anxiety are in a constant state of fight or flight. If they fear that they are in danger, then they may act aggressively to protect themselves or may run in order to stay safe. Without knowledge of the underlying reason for the behavior, a child-care provider who does not associate aggression with anxiety may become frustrated with the child. This is how anxiety can lead to expulsion. If the program feels the child causes a threat to others in the classroom, then she may be asked to leave the program. However, if the family and child-care provider can work to alleviate the child's anxiety, then there would be no potential threat.

SUPPORTING STEVEN

Shelby is the mother of three children: Ava, Joshua, and Steven. Ava, the oldest child, enjoys going to school and always demonstrates her best work. Joshua is an example of what many people call "pure boy." He is obsessed with sports and enjoys going to elementary school to hang out with all of his friends. Joshua was diagnosed with a physical disability when he was younger, and he underwent several years of physical therapy. He did have an IEP in preschool so that he could attend public preschool and receive special-education support, but as he grew, he overcame a lot of the challenges associated with the disability. He did not need continued special-education support to be successful in the classroom and complete his work. He was easily completing grade-level assignments and seemed happy in the classroom.

Shelby's youngest son, Steven, is very different from her older children. Of course, everyone's children differ from one another, but Steven's overall development seems significantly different from his siblings'. Shelby had been a public elementary school teacher before she decided to stay home with her children, so she has a good working knowledge of when children should be able to achieve certain developmental goals. Steven doesn't seem to be meeting those goals in the same path that his brother and sister had met them. Steven is definitely smart, but it seems like his mind and his body never stop moving. It is hard to get him to slow down long enough to take in information. He isn't able to process an instruction or directions the same way that his siblings can because he is always moving at light speed.

When Ava and Joshua were preschool aged, they attended a part-time preschool in a church close to Shelby's neighborhood. When Steven was approximately two years old, Shelby filled out an application for him to attend the program starting when he was about two-and-a-half. As they waited for him to enroll, Shelby was working toward re-entering the workforce. She had applied for teacher and assistant-teacher positions in the public school system. Luckily, she had family members who lived in the same town, so if she wanted to substitute teach or work part-time, a grandparent could watch Steven for a day or an afternoon. Shelby's goal was to get a full-time teacher position again, but the school system was so competitive that she would have to work her way back into a position.

When it was finally time for Steven to start at the church preschool, he was so excited, but of course Steven was excited about everything. As Ava and Joshua prepared to start another year of elementary school, Steven was going to go to preschool like a big boy. Unfortunately, the beginning of the new school year did not turn out as Shelby had anticipated. Two weeks after Steven started preschool, the program director asked Shelby not to bring him back. The director said that Steven was "not a good fit for the program."

Of course, Shelby was overwhelmed by this information. She was embarrassed that her son did not seem to meet the preschool's expectations of how a child should behave. She questioned the parenting skills of herself and her husband. Their first two children had not behaved like this. Had she slacked off on discipline because Steven was her third child? Or was this just Steven and he would always be a wild card? If this was just who Steven was, would other schools also tell him that he was not a "good fit"? How long would it take Steven to understand that the schools didn't want him there?

Many questions were racing through her head, but Shelby had to put a plan together. She needed to talk to their pediatrician and see if she had concerns about Steven. She needed to find another child-care program for Steven, because she was now working in a school full-time. Her mother had been watching Steven in the afternoons, but it would be a lot for her to have to watch him the full day. Shelby also needed to see if she could get Steven some help.

Shelby had a friend whose son had also struggled in preschool and had exhibited some of the same behaviors as Steven. Joshua played on the same baseball team as Helen's son, and when Shelby watched Jack now, he didn't seem to have any of the problems that Helen had told her about when Jack was younger. Shelby wondered exactly what type of support Helen had gotten for Jack.

While Shelby was watching a baseball game with Helen, she started asking her a lot of questions, such as when Helen first noticed that Jack was not developing like other children and what the doctor had recommended. Helen had worked as a special-education teacher, so she gave Shelby information about specialists in the area who worked with preschool-age children and about the types of therapy that Jack had received. Helen told Shelby about a group of pediatric occupational therapists who had done an amazing job helping Jack, but Helen warned Shelby that this therapy practice did not take medical insurance, so the costs could mount up quickly.

Shelby arranged for Steven to start occupational therapy. She also started looking for another preschool. Several friends told her about a preschool their children went to that they had loved. Shelby looked at several other preschool programs, but eventually she selected the program that her friends had recommended.

Instead of being blindsided again, Shelby decided to be up front with the child-care program director and let her know that Steven had struggled at the last program. During the tour of the new preschool, Shelby asked detailed questions about the center's policy on toilet training, their social expectations for the children, their behavior-management system, and what daily routines they used in the classroom. She explained that she had found an occupational therapist (OT) to evaluate Steven and that their family would work with the child-care program to help his transition into a new classroom go as smoothly as possible. Steven did not have a diagnosis at that time, but Shelby tried to explain the behaviors that he was exhibiting to help the director understand what type of support he would need.

The director of the preschool was willing to work out a plan with Shelby to help Steven be more successful. Shelby had worked with the OT to plan for her to come to the child-care center and train the teachers on how best to work with Steven. This was especially helpful once Steven had been officially diagnosed with sensory processing disorder. The OT recommended strategies to help calm him down or help him seek the sensory information that his body needed without being disruptive to the rest of the children in the classroom. Helen had been right about the OT: she was expensive (causing a little bit of a strain on the family budget), but she was amazing at what she did. She was just strict enough with Steven that he responded to all her requests, but she was personable enough that he developed a strong attachment to her. Of course, one hour of occupational therapy each week was not enough time with the OT to eliminate all the negative behaviors that Steven was demonstrating, so that meant the teachers and his family would have to do much of the work themselves.

At first, the plan with the center director seemed to be working out. The director was communicating with Shelby frequently and trying to make the needed classroom adaptations. After a while, though, the classroom staff became overwhelmed with caring for Steven. They had determined that one staff member would always have to be with Steven, so the other teacher in the classroom ended up having to care for all the other children in the classroom by herself. That was a lot of work for one teacher.

Shelby was attempting to follow every recommendation that the OT offered. She had found a weighted blanket to help him slow down at night and get a deep sleep so that his body would be more under control the next day at school. She had started using bear hugs and other deep-pressure techniques to help him calm down when he seemed to be moving too fast to slow his mind and body down. However, all these suggestions were not making as much progress as the preschool desired.

The preschool director scheduled a meeting with Shelby and her husband to talk about their plan for Steven. When they arrived, they realized the true purpose of the meeting was to tell them that Steven needed to find a different preschool. The meeting was scheduled for mid-December, not too long before the winter break, and the director told Shelby and her husband that Steven could not return again in January. Shelby's mother would be able to help out for a while, but she could not do this long term. Also, Steven needed help to learn to function in a classroom setting before he started kindergarten, so that he would have the opportunity to focus on academics instead of on controlling his body. The preschool did make a final offer that Steven could continue to attend if he had a parent with him at all times, but for two working parents, this offer was not helpful. Shelby withdrew Steven from his second preschool program and began to search for another solution.

By this point, Shelby was working full time as a para-educator at Ava and Joshua's school, where there was a public preschool program. To attend, Steven would have to qualify through the screening process, and Shelby would have to find somewhere for him to be each afternoon because the preschool program was only three hours per day. Shelby contacted the central office for the school district, and she asked to set up an evaluation for Steven. The preschool diagnostician used several different types of evaluation kits to collect all the information that he needed, and then the family had to wait for over a month to find out if Steven qualified.

Once they finally received the news that he could attend public preschool, they were thrilled. He would be in the same building each day as his mother, sister, and brother. He would have a teacher with a master's degree in early childhood special education and extensive experience working with children like Steven. He would also get the benefit of being in the classroom with speech pathologists, occupational therapists, and behavior specialists as they worked with all the different children in the classroom. All these resources would be beneficial for Steven.

The downside of all this good news was that, once again, Steven did not have afternoon child care. Shelby's mother had always been so gracious to help when needed, but as Steven's behavior got a little more out of control, Shelby's mother admitted that it was harder for her to take care of him. Luckily, if she picked up Steven from school at 10:30 a.m., there would not be much time left before he needed to eat lunch and take a nap. As fast as Steven moved around throughout the day, he had always been a good napper. When he woke up in the afternoon, it wouldn't be too long until Shelby could come and pick him up. By staying home with his grandmother, Steven also had the opportunity to see his regular OT once a week. This new opportunity would give Steven a year and a half of public preschool before starting kindergarten, and hopefully, he would be more prepared to enter kindergarten successfully.

Shelby was grateful for how her situation had turned out, but she continued to worry about other children whose parents' schedules would not allow them to attend half-day special-education preschool. Where did those children go to preschool? Were they kicked out of multiple preschools like Steven had been? Or did they find a preschool that supported children with special needs but have to go into debt to afford to send their children? All children with disabilities should have access to high-quality child care, regardless of whether they can afford to pay a high fee, and child-care programs should have the supports in place to let any child attend, regardless of a disability.

Chapter 11: A Call to Action

After thoroughly looking at all aspects of the child-care system, it is easy to see why the system is failing. No business can spend more money than it takes in and expect to continue. No employer can pay its employees a small salary for a large workload and expect those staff members to stay in their positions for an extended period of time. No employee wants to work for low wages and also be disrespected by the community, in spite of his hard work. No teacher wants to try to work with a classroom full of students, feeling defeated every day and with only limited resources.

Despite these circumstances, parents need child care in order to work. Most families need all the adults in the home to help support the household. Children who attend public school during the day still need after-school care for two to three hours before their families can pick them up. Children with special needs must have highly trained teachers in their classrooms who can help them be as successful as possible.

All these problems and needs were present before the COVID-19 pandemic; however, once the pandemic crippled the child-care industry by closing down centers all across America, the problems now seem insurmountable. State and federal funding has been dispersed to child-care programs across the country, but that effort is only patching a broken system. The true answer to these problems is complete systemic change.

Now is the time to rethink what does not work and to completely overhaul the system. Most child-care programs will not be able to sustain themselves through the first twelve to eighteen months after the pandemic, unless more significant support is offered. States have reduced center capacity, and parents are timid about returning their children to group care. The child-care programs do not have the same financial support that they have had in the past. The United States must step back and decide what infrastructure changes must be made to preserve this industry for years to come. In particular, we must change public opinion of the early child-care field, fund private child care, encourage the growth of private child-care homes, get business buy-in, and meet the needs of exceptional children.

CHANGE PUBLIC OPINION OF THE FIELD

It is obvious that child care does not get the attention it needs from the government or the community. To receive support, it is essential to validate the profession. The main way to show the importance and significance of child care is to demonstrate that child-care providers are valued professionals. They must be paid more. They must be paid a salary that shows the importance of their work and the depth of their workload. A child-care provider's salary needs to be comparable to that of a K-12 school teacher, because the job responsibilities are similar. If pay rates are increased, child-care programs will have the opportunity to hire highly trained early childhood professionals. If those professionals receive a fair salary with benefits, they will be more likely to stay in their positions and provide consistent care for children. So many of the systemic issues with child care relate to high expectations and low pay. This issue can be repeated over and over again, but the end result will still be that early child-care programs will not be valued until the child-care providers who work in them are valued. This must be the first step to change.

A second step to changing public perception is a strong consumer-education campaign based outside federal or state governments. Many communities also appreciate hearing the data-driven perspectives of independent nonprofit organizations that are free from political affiliation. This means that child-advocacy organizations, professional medical organizations, education unions, and nonprofit organizations need to band together to offer a concise and unified opinion on the importance of early childhood education. Such an effort may involve social-media campaigns, op-ed pieces in local newspapers or on digital bulletin boards, and blogs and podcasts.

In addition, a stronger relationship is needed between early child care and departments of education throughout the United States. Although the K-12 school system values child care, it often does not feel that child care is as valuable as elementary and secondary school. This discrimination is evident in the campaign by teachers' unions to close K-12 schools during COVID-19 to protect the health of the teachers, but not campaign on behalf of teachers in child-care programs. In fact, many elementary schools have expected child care to be open to support the children who cannot attend school during these closures. Contributing to the perception of child care as a supplement to "real school" are the poor working relationships between the child-care industry and the public education system as well as a misconception about what child-care providers actually do. If elementary teachers could see the developmental assessments, emergent curriculum, and social-emotional guidance provided by high-quality child-care programs, their perception might change dramatically. The partnership between child care and public education needs to begin by taking a deeper look at the hard work of the child-care providers.

Another way to improve public perception of the field is a continued emphasis on higher education. Child-care providers in many states can enter the field with a high school diploma or a GED. However, many different opportunities exist for additional education. For example, Head Start asks for all assistant teachers to have a Child Development Associate's degree, also known as a CDA. This credential, offered through the Council for Professional Recognition, is equivalent to approximately two college courses and gives newer teachers the opportunity to learn about child development, curriculum, assessment, and working with parents. Many community colleges and universities now offer programs in early childhood education or early childhood special education, and they also offer associate's and bachelor's degrees in the field, based on the interest of the student. Child-care providers who pursue higher education not only have more knowledge on how to support children in the classroom but also continue to change the public perception of what a child-care provider should be because of their professional advancement.

Finally, to change public perception of child care, parents must be educated about what quality child care is. This is a consumer-education effort that many states have already started with the introduction of quality rating systems for child-care programs. Despite massive marketing efforts, many parents still select child care based on recommendations from friends or family members, instead of searching for a high-quality program. Parents need education on the benefits of developmental assessments and how quality programs can use that information to create lesson plans to help children develop to their fullest potential. Of course, quality child-care programs do some of this marketing themselves, but it is also important for other community partners to be involved in this process, since many families may not have access to this information.

DISBURSE STATE AND FEDERAL DOLLARS TO THE PRIVATE SECTOR

In the past, federal dollars for child-care programs have focused on making sure that the most vulnerable children have access to quality child care. The COVID-19 virus, however, most severely affected child-care programs that do not receive federal subsidies. Now all children are in desperate need of stable child care, regardless of their socioeconomic status. This means that distribution of federal and state financial supports must cover a broader range of child-care programs, both in child-care centers and in family child-care homes.

The federal government and individual states offer significant funding to K-12 education and higher-education programs. We now know that early education has a profound effect on a child's progress through elementary school. We also know that child care is costing families more than higher education (CCA of America, 2019). Therefore, it is time that federal and state governments view high-quality child care as essential, in the same way they view high-quality elementary school. An increase in funding for child care can have a dramatic influence on the pay rate for child-care providers, thereby attracting early education professionals who are well trained and experienced in working with our youngest children. It is essential that the federal government and states increase funding from multiple streams to benefit our child-care programs.

The purposes of government funding for child care also need to be re-evaluated. In the past, most funding has gone toward supporting low-income families so that they can afford consistent child care, thereby potentially reducing the number of families living in poverty. Of course, this is still an essential use of child-care funding. However, the COVID-19 pandemic has placed an immediate focus on a larger issue: the economy. Federal and state funds need to be directed at keeping the entire child-care system open long term.

Without child care, the economy cannot survive.

The goals in every state should be to preserve as much child-care capacity as possible and to increase quality nationwide. As more centers and family child-care homes close their doors, there are fewer and fewer available spots for children to attend child care. If fewer children can attend child care, then fewer parents can work. It is as simple as that. Without child care, the economy cannot survive. Stabilizing child-care capacity should be the predominant goal for the next few years to make sure that the system does not collapse.

Block-grant funding and state-budget funds, which focus on the centers that are most commonly used by children who receive a child-care subsidy, need additional flexibility to support all child-care programs. Of course, children in low-income families need to receive subsidized child care, and children with special needs should also receive subsidies to make sure that they can attend high-quality programs that can support their needs. Programs should also receive financial incentives for demonstrating elevated levels of quality as assessed by their state quality rating systems or through national accreditation programs.

PRIORITIZE THE GROWTH OF FAMILY CHILD-CARE HOMES

As states look to maintain necessary capacity for all the families who need child care, they also need to think about how to increase the number of family child-care homes. These in-home providers offer the most flexible schedules for care, including evening and weekend care, and they offer the small, mixed-age environment that many families are looking for as their children re-enter group child care. Plus, family child-care homes can sustain their businesses in areas where centers cannot get enough enrollment due to the distance between families or the cost of commercial property. With the dramatic decrease that the United States has seen in family child-care homes since 2005, it is essential to recruit and prioritize resources around these providers as the nation attempts to maintain child-care capacity.

A way to support family child-care homes is to change the zoning laws that prohibit these types of small businesses from operating in neighborhoods. Family child-care homes are not the same as storefront businesses. They preserve the feeling of the neighborhood, but they also support the families within the neighborhood. They allow children to have a loving child-care setting in a regulated home that has been inspected for health and safety measures. Many counties throughout the United States have established laws that prohibit family child-care homes in their neighborhoods, and it is one of the reasons that we are losing this type of child care.

Start-up grants from government agencies or foundations could go a long way toward helping providers purchase a business computer, cribs, fencing, or safety materials such as door gates and cabinet locks. Many providers also need assistance learning how to upgrade their homeowner's insurance and pay their annual zoning fees. With a small amount of coaching and initial start-up grants, more individuals may be interested in starting their own professional businesses.

Another way to support family child-care homes is by offering additional field coaching in how to operate a business. Family child-care providers need training in how to establish the cost of care at their facilities, how to create a budget, and how to file their annual taxes. If providers can set up a strong business framework, then they are much more likely to keep their businesses open long term.

Family child-care homes also need access to field coaching and training that is directed to their needs. Most training agencies set up their trainings to target center-based child care, simply because they can attract a larger audience that way. Because there are more center-based employees, it is easier to get full enrollment. Some of these trainings, such as general child development or training on the CACFP, can apply to family child-care homes; however, curriculum-based training is very different in a child-care home. Providers need coaching on how to run a quality home program rather than on what a center should look like. In-home providers need assistance in understanding how to work with different age groups at the same time, how to set up a home environment for learning, and how one child-care provider can implement all these varied skills independently. Training agencies could find new ways to utilize virtual home tours for helping with room arrangements, and they could form a network of family child-care home providers to support one another.

GET BUSINESS BUY-IN

The business community really has the most vested interest in making sure that working parents can access the quality child care they need. Businesses suffer when parents must leave the workforce. They must hire new, untrained employees and hope they stay at the company long enough to justify the initial investment in the orientation training. The COVID-19 pandemic has shown many employers how essential child care is for their business functions, so now is the best time to support the needs of employees and business productivity as well.

One model for supporting employees is offering on-site child care. If employers have available space for a child-care program, they can choose to manage the program themselves or find an outside agency to manage the center. On-site child care allows the center to remain open whenever the company is open, even if the company does not have traditional business hours. For example, the Toyota plant in Georgetown, Kentucky, has a twenty-four-hour child-care program to support employees, regardless of which shift they work. An employer can offer the child care as an employee benefit to attract talent who may be searching for nontraditional benefits.

Other businesses may not be large enough to have their own child-care program or may not have the space for child care on their property. An option for them would be to partner with a local child-care center or create a child-care network for their employees. This can look very different, depending on the size of the company and the employees' needs. For example, a small business may want to partner with a local child-care center and ask the program to reserve slots for their employees' children. The business can provide a financial stipend to the center to reserve the designated number of slots, and then the employer can refer new employees to enroll their children at that center. Some larger companies may want to participate in a child-care network to give their employees choices in the child-care selection process. For example, the employer may reach out to two centers and three family child-care homes in the area to establish the network. A financial agreement can be established to give the employees first priority at available openings in the child-care programs. The employer may also request that the child-care programs maintain a certain level of accreditation or certain hours of operation to meet the needs of the employees. A company employing many parents who work nights and weekends may want to partner solely with family child-care homes to make sure that all employees have access to child care during nontraditional hours.

Employers can also support the child-care industry by offering a stipend to eligible employees each month that can be spent at the child-care center of the employee's choice. The stipend would not cover the full cost of care, but it would allow employees to afford higher-quality child care than they could pay for on their own. Some companies offer this stipend through a reimbursement process or a flex spending account. If parents can afford to pay for higher-quality child care, then quality child-care programs are more likely to maintain full enrollment.

SUPPORT EXCEPTIONAL CHILDREN

It is also essential for the United States to begin thinking about the essential nature of quality child care for children with special needs. Children with disabilities do not simply begin to need full-time care once they arrive at kindergarten. And the families of children with disabilities are more likely to need every adult in the house to work in order to afford the best possible health insurance and to pay for additional expenses. Families of children with disabilities do not need to go to work each day wondering how long they will be at their desks before the child-care program calls and tells them to pick up their child. Reliable, inclusive child care is extremely important. Child-care providers must get key coaching and training to support children with special needs. Child-care providers need to partner with the public school system and Head Start programs to gain access to essential special-education trainings offered by therapists and diagnosticians.

If child-care providers must offer specialized care, then their salaries need to reflect the fact that they are specialists. Working with children who have disabilities is a high-turnover field, even in the public school system. Teachers are often overwhelmed, so child-care programs need to compensate their teachers accordingly for their experience and education. With increased compensation, tuition for programs that support special needs will be higher. It will be essential for foundations and governments to subsidize child care for children with special needs so they can get all the support they need.

CHILD CARE AT A CROSSROADS

Now is the time for America to decide to support child care. Child care benefits our economy. It benefits our children and our families. Whole communities benefit when children are in safe, high-quality early childhood settings. It is no longer possible for businesses and government to say that child care is a personal matter that does not concern them. Child care concerns everyone, and changes must be made now.

REFERENCES AND RECOMMENDED READING

Adam, Gina, and Margaret Todd. 2020. "Meeting the School-Age Child Care Needs of Working Parents Facing COVID-19 Distance Learning: Policy Options to Consider." Working paper. Urban Institute. https://www.urban.org/sites/default/files/publication/102621/meeting-the-school-age-child-care-needs-of-working-parents-facing-covid-19-distance-learning.pdf

Afterschool Alliance. 2014. *America after 3 pm: Afterschool Programs in Demand.* Afterschool Alliance. https://www.afterschoolalliance.org/documents/AA3PM-2014/AA3PM_Key_Findings.pdf

Afterschool Alliance. 2020. "Issue: School-Age Child Care: Afterschool Programs Are a Critical Resource to Working Parents." Afterschool Alliance. https://www.afterschoolalliance.org/Issue-School-Age-Child-Care.cfm

American Academy of Pediatrics. 2018. "Child Abuse and Neglect." HealthyChildren.org. https://www.healthychildren.org/English/safety-prevention/at-home/Pages/What-to-Know-about-Child-Abuse.aspx

American Academy of Pediatrics. 2020a. "COVID-19 Planning Considerations: Guidance for School Re-Entry." American Academy of Pediatrics. https://services.aap.org/en/pages/2019-novel-coronavirus-covid-19-infections/clinical-guidance/covid-19-planning-considerations-return-to-in-person-education-in-schools/

American Academy of Pediatrics. 2020b. "Nutrition." HealthyChildren.org. https://www.healthychildren.org/English/healthy-living/nutrition/Pages/default.aspx

Belfield, Clive R. 2018. *The Economic Impacts of Insufficient Child Care on Working Families.* Washington, DC: ReadyNation/Council for a Strong America. https://strongnation.s3.amazonaws.com/documents/522/3c5cdb46-eda2–4723–9e8e-f20511cc9f0f.pdf?1542205790andinline; percent20filename=percent22The percent20Economic percent20Impacts percent200f percent20Insufficient percent20Child percent20Care percent200n percent20Working percent20Families.pdf percent22

Blair, Clancy, and C. Cybele Raver. 2016. "Poverty, Stress, and Brain Development: New Directions for Prevention and Intervention." *Academic Pediatrics* 16(3): 30–36.

Bui, Quoctrung, and Claire Cain Miller. 2018. "The Age That Women Have Babies: How a Gap Divides America." *The New York Times*, August 4. https://www.nytimes.com/interactive/2018/08/04/upshot/up-birth-age-gap. html#:~:text=The%20average%20age%20of%20first%2Dtime%20mothers%20 is%2026%2C%20up,of%20first%20birth%20is%2031

Bureau of Labor Statistics (US Department of Labor). 2018. Occupational Employment Statistics (OES) tables.

Butrymowicz, Sarah, and Jackie Mader. 2016. "High Turnover and Low Pay for Employees May Undermine State's Child Care System." The Hechinger Report. https://hechingerreport.org/high-turnover-and-low-pay-for-employees-may-undermine-states-child-care-system/

Center on the Developing Child. 2020. "In Brief: The Science of Early Childhood Development." Center on the Developing Child, Harvard University. https://developingchild.harvard.edu/resources/inbrief-science-of-ecd/

Centers for Disease Control and Prevention. 2020a. "The Importance of Reopening America's Schools This Fall." CDC.gov. https://www.cdc.gov/coronavirus/2019-ncov/community/schools-childcare/reopening-schools.html

Centers for Disease Control and Prevention. 2020b. "People at Increased Risk." CDC.gov. https://www.cdc.gov/coronavirus/2019-ncov/need-extra-precautions/index.html

Centers for Disease Control and Prevention. 2020c. "Symptoms of Coronavirus." CDC.gov. https://www.cdc.gov/coronavirus/2019-ncov/symptoms-testing/symptoms.html

Child Care Aware of America. 2019. "The US and the High Price of Child Care: An Examination of a Broken System." Child Care Aware of America. https://usa.childcareaware.org/priceofcare

ChildCare.gov. 2020. "Family Child-Care Homes." US Department of Health and Human Services, Administration for Children and Families, Office of Child Care. https://www.childcare.gov/consumer-education/family-child-care-homes

Children's Bureau. 2019. *Mandatory Reporters of Child Abuse and Neglect.* Washington, DC: US Department of Health and Human Services, Administration for Children and Families, Administration on Children, Youth, and Families, Children's Bureau. https://www.childwelfare.gov/pubPDFs/manda.pdf

Committee for Economic Development. 2019. *Child Care in State Econo-mies—2019 Updates.* Committee for Economic Development of the Confer-ence Board. https://www.ced.org/childcareimpact

Conger, Dylan, et al. 2019. "New Benefits of Public School Pre-Kindergar-ten Programs: Early School Stability, Grade Promotion, and Exit from ELL Services." *Early Childhood Research Quarterly* 48(3): 26–35.

Coronavirus Aid, Relief, and Economic Security Act, S.3548, 116th Congress. 2020. https://www.congress.gov/bill/116th-congress/senate-bill/3548

Davis, Belinda, et al. 2017. *Losing Ground: How Child Care Impacts Louisiana's Workforce Productivity and the State Economy.* New Orleans, LA: Louisiana Policy Institute for Children, Entergy, Louisiana State University Public Policy Research Lab. http://www.brylskicompany.com/uploads/1/7/4/0/17400267/losing_ground-1.pdf

Early Childhood Training and Technical Assistance System. 2018. *Fundamentals of CCDF Administration Resource Guide.* Washington, DC: US Department of Health and Human Services, Administration for Children and Families, Office of Child Care. https://ccdf-fundamentals.icfcloud.com/sites/default/files/public/pdf/CCDF percent20Fundamentals percent20Resource percent20Guide.pdf

Fraga, Lynette. 2020. "Coronavirus Calculation: No Child Care, No Econom-ic Recovery." Fox Business. https://www.foxbusiness.com/markets/coronavirus-child-care-economic-recovery

First Five Years Fund. 2019. "Preschool Development Grant Birth through Five (PDG B–5)." First Five Years Fund. https://www.ffyf.org/issues/pdg/

Goldberg, Emma. 2020. "The Pandemic's Setbacks for Working Moms." *The New York Times,* July 2. https://www.nytimes.com/2020/07/02/insider/virus-working-moms.html

Goldberg, Hana, Tim Cairl, and Thomas J. Cunningham. 2018. *Opportunities Lost: How Child Care Challenges Affect Georgia's Workforce and Economy.* Atlanta, GA: Georgia Early Education Alliance for Ready Students, Metro Atlanta Chamber. https://www.metroatlantachamber.com/assets/opportunities-lost-report-final_ymXE7Za.pdf

Gorsky, Laura. 2018. "Expulsions in Early Childhood Hurt Infants, Toddlers, and Their Families." National Women's Law Center. https://nwlc.org/blog/ expulsions-in-early-childhood-hurt-infants-toddlers-and-their-families/

Gould, Elise. 2015. "Child Care Workers Aren't Paid Enough to Make Ends Meet." Economic Policy Institute. https://www.epi.org/publication/ child-care-workers-arent-paid-enough-to-make-ends-meet/

Gould, Elise, and Hunter Blair. 2020. *Who's Paying Now? The Explicit and Implicit Cost of the Current Early Care and Education System.* Economic Policy Institute. https://www.epi.org/publication/whos-paying-now-costs-of-the-current-ece-system/

Head Start Early Childhood Learning and Knowledge Center. 2020. "Understanding and Eliminating Expulsion in Early Childhood Programs." US Department of Health and Human Services, Administration for Children and Families. https://eclkc.ohs.acf.hhs.gov/publication/understanding-eliminating-expulsion-early-childhood-programs

Henley, Julia R., and Gina Adams. 2018. *Insights on Access to Quality Child Care for Children with Disabilities and Special Needs.* Washington, DC: Urban Institute. https://www.urban.org/sites/default/files/publication/99146/ insights_on_access_to_quality_child_care_for_children_with_disabilities_and_ special_needs_0.pdf

Honig, Alice Sterling. 2014. *The Best for Babies: Expert Advice for Assessing Infant-Toddler Programs.* Lewisville, NC: Gryphon House.

Johns Hopkins Medicine. 2020. "Coronavirus Disease 2019 vs. the Flu." Johns Hopkins Medicine. https://www.hopkinsmedicine.org/health/ conditions-and-diseases/coronavirus/coronavirus-disease-2019-vs-the-flu

Johnson, Andrea, et al. 2018. *Stepping Up: New Policies and Strategies Supporting Parents in Low-Wage Jobs and Their Children.* Washington, DC: National Women's Law Center. https://nwlc-ciw49tixgw51bab.stackpathdns.com/ wp-content/uploads/2018/08/v2_final_nwlc_SteppingUpKelloggReport.pdf

Littlepage, Laura. 2018. *Lost Opportunities: The Impact of Inadequate Child Care on Indiana's Workforce and Economy.* Indianapolis, IN: Indiana University Public Policy Institute. https://earlylearningin.org/wp-content/uploads/2018/10/ economic.impact_early.learning_sep.28.2018_final.pdf

Mader, Jackie. 2020. "Where Do Kids with Disabilities Go for Childcare?" The Hechinger Report. https://hechingerreport.org/where-do-kids-with-disabilities-go-for-child-care/

Malik, Rasheed. 2019. "Working Families Are Spending Big Money on Childcare." Center on American Progress. https://cdn.americanprogress.org/content/uploads/2019/06/19074131/Working-Families-SpendingBRIEF.pdf?_ga=2.211079701.1232102200.1597592885–33191074.1596843656

Malik, Rasheed, and Katie Hamm. 2017. *Mapping America's Child Care Deserts*. Center on American Progress. https://www.americanprogress.org/issues/early-childhood/reports/2017/08/30/437988/mapping-americas-child-care-deserts/

Malik, Rasheed, et al. 2018. *America's Child Care Deserts in 2018*. Center for American Progress. https://www.americanprogress.org/issues/early-childhood/reports/2018/12/06/461643/americas-child-care-deserts-2018/

McKenna, Aileen. 2010. "Reluctant to Report: The Mandated Reporting Practices of Child-Care providers." Doctoral diss. Kalamazoo, MI: Western Michigan University. https://scholarworks.wmich.edu/cgi/viewcontent.cgi?referer=andhttpsredir=1andarticle=1439andcontext=dissertations

McLean, Caitlin. 2020. "What's Causing the Shortage of Qualified Early Care and Education Teachers? There's a Hole in the Bucket." Center for the Study of Child Care Employment. https://cscce.berkeley.edu/hole-in-the-bucket/

Mongeau, Lillian. 2018. "Who Should Pay for Preschool for the Middle Class?" The Hechinger Report. https://hechingerreport.org/who-should-pay-for-preschool/

National Association for the Education of Young Children. 2020. *Child Care in Crisis: Understanding the Effects of the Coronavirus Pandemic*. Washington, DC: National Association for the Education of Young Children. https://www.naeyc.org/sites/default/files/globally-shared/downloads/PDFs/our-work/public-policy-advocacy/effects_of_coronavirus_on_child_care.final.pdf

National Center on Early Childhood Quality Assurance. 2019. *Addressing the Decreasing Number of Family Child-care providers in the United States*. Fairfax, VA: National Center on Early Childhood Quality Assurance, US Department of Health and Human Services, Administration for Children and Families. https://childcareta.acf.hhs.gov/sites/default/files/public/addressing_decreasing_fcc_providers_revised_final.pdf

National Women's Law Center. 2017. "Child Care Is Out of Reach for Many Low Income Families, New NWLC Report Shows." National Women's Law Center. https://nwlc.org/press-releases/child-care-is-out-of-reach-for-many-low-income-families-new-nwlc-report-shows/

Novoa, Cristina. 2020. *The Child Care Crisis Disproportionately Affects Children with Disabilities*. Center for American Progress. https://www.americanprogress.org/issues/early-childhood/reports/2020/01/29/479802/child-care-crisis-disproportionately-affects-children-disabilities/

Novoa, Cristina, and Rasheed Malik. 2018. *Suspensions Are Not Support*. Center for American Progress. https://www.americanprogress.org/issues/early-childhood/reports/2018/01/17/445041/suspensions-not-support/

Office of Child Care. 2012. "CCDF Final Regulations." US Department of Health and Human Services, Administration for Children and Familes. https://www.acf.hhs.gov/occ/resource/ccdf-final-regulations#:~:text=CCDF%20State%20Match%20Provisions%20Final,of%20CCDF%20Federal%20matching%20funds.

Office of Child Care. 2019. "The Decreasing Number of Family Child-Care Providers in the United States." US Department of Health and Human Services, Administration for Children and Families. https://www.acf.hhs.gov/occ/news/the-decreasing-number-of-family-child-care-providers-in-the-united-states

Office of Child Care. 2020. "About." US Department of Health and Human Services, Administration for Children and Families. https://www.acf.hhs.gov/occ/about

Office of Early Learning. n.d. "Voluntary Prekindergarten." Office of Early Learning, Florida Department of Education. http://www.floridaearlylearning.com/vpk

Office of Head Start. 2019. "The History of Head Start." US Department of Health and Human Services, Administration for Children and Families. https://www.acf.hhs.gov/ohs/about/history-of-head-start

Power, Denise. 2019. "The Millennial Mindset: Employee Benefits for the World's Largest Generation." US Chamber of Commerce. https://www.uschamber.com/co/run/human-resources/employee-benefits-millennials

Powers, Lindsay. 2020. "Why I Paid $50,000 for a Year of Child Care." *The New York Times*, February 14. https://www.nytimes.com/2020/02/14/parenting/childcare-costs.html

Prichard Committee for Academic Excellence. 2017. *Building Blocks: The Kentucky Early Childhood Cost of Quality Study*. Lexington, KY: Prichard Committee for Academic Excellence. http://prichardcommittee.org/wp-content/uploads/Cost-of-Quality-Brief-November-2017.pdf

Rachidi, Angela. 2019. "How Do Low-Income Families Pay for Child Care?" American Enterprise Institute. https://www.aei.org/poverty-studies/how-do-low-income-families-pay-for-child-care/

Schochet, Leila. 2019. *The Child Care Crisis Is Keeping Women Out of the Workforce*. Center for American Progress. https://www.americanprogress.org/issues/early-childhood/reports/2019/03/28/467488/child-care-crisis-keeping-women-workforce/

Schulman, Karen. 2019. *Early Progress: State Child Care Assistance Policies 2019*. Washington, DC: National Women's Law Center. https://nwlc-ciw49tixgw51bab.stackpathdns.com/wp-content/uploads/2019/11/NWLC-State-Child-Care-Assistance-Policies-2019-final.pdf

Shpancer, Noam. 2019. "Choosing Childcare: What Should Parents Look For?" *Psychology Today*. https://www.psychologytoday.com/us/blog/insight-therapy/201908/choosing-childcare-what-should-parents-look

Stanton, Zack. 2020. "How the Child Care Crisis Will Distort the Economy for a Generation." *Politico*. https://www.politico.com/news/magazine/2020/07/23/child-care-crisis-pandemic-economy-impact-women-380412

Stoney, Louise. 2010. "The Iron Triangle: A Simple Formula for Financial Policy in ECE Programs." *Exchange Every Day*. https://www.childcareexchange.com/eed/issue/2650/

Thomason, Sarah, et al. 2018. "At the Wage Floor: Covering Homecare and Early Care and Education Workers in the New Generation of Minimum Wage Laws." Center for the Study of Child Care Employment, University of California at Berkeley. https://cscce.berkeley.edu/at-the-wage-floor/

Ullrich, Rebecca, and Aaron Sojourner. 2020. *Child Care Is Key to Our Economic Recovery*. The Center for Law and Social Policy. https://www.clasp.org/publications/report/brief/child-care-key-our-economic-recovery

US Chamber of Commerce Foundation. 2020. *Employers, Childcare, and Returning to Work in COVID-19*. US Chamber of Commerce Foundation. https://www.uschamberfoundation.org/reports/covid-19-impact-childcare

US Department of Agriculture. 2019. "FNS 101: Child and Adult Care Food Program." US Department of Agriculture, Food and Nutrition Service. https://www.fns.usda.gov/fns-101-cacfp

US Department of Health and Human Services. 2012. "What Is TANF?" HHS. gov. https://www.hhs.gov/answers/programs-for-families-and-children/what-is-tanf/index.html

US Department of Health and Human Services, US Department of Education. 2013. "Race to the Top: Early Learning Challenge." https://www2.ed.gov/programs/racetothetop-earlylearningchallenge/2013-early-learning-challenge-flyer.pdf

Vanover, Sarah T. 2016. "Family Preferences for Childcare in Central Kentucky." Doctoral diss. Richmond, KY: Eastern Kentucky University. Online Theses and Dissertations. 442. https://encompass.eku.edu/etd/442

Workman, Simon, and Steven Jessen-Howard. 2018. *Understanding the True Cost of Child Care for Infants and Toddlers*. Center for American Progress. https://www.americanprogress.org/issues/early-childhood/reports/2018/11/15/460970/understanding-true-cost-child-care-infants-toddlers/

Workman, Simon, and Steven Jessen-Howard. 2019. *Conducting a Child Care Cost of Quality Study: A Toolkit for States and Communities*. Washington, DC: Center for American Progress. https://www.thencit.org/sites/default/files/2019-03/Cost%20of%20Quality%20Toolkit.pdf

INDEX

A

Adult-to-child ratio, 17, 27–28, 58–59, 73–74, 120, 122, 125–126

Affordability vs. cost, 3–4, 10, 13–2, 58–59

After-school care, 92–94, 133

American Academy of Pediatrics, 8, 107, 110

Americans with Disabilities Act, 121–122

B

Background checks, 46, 48, 60, 71–72, 109

Benefits, 10, 17, 19–21, 28–29

Block-grant funding, 136–137

Bureau of Labor Statistics, 2–3, 85

Business community
    benefits of child care, 83–84
    buy-in, 138–139
    employer perspective, 87–90
    impact of child care, 1–2, 81–90
    reopening after COVID–19, 84–87
    state and national perspectives, 82–83

C

Center for American Progress, 14, 58, 62, 69

Centers for Disease Control and Prevention, 5, 7–8, 109

Challenging behaviors, 38, 73, 121, 125

Child abuse, 101, 105–109, 115, 126

Child and Adult Care Food Program, 105, 110–113

Child Care and Development Block Grant, 10, 45–50, 52, 93, 96

Child Care and Development Funding State Match Provisions Final Rule, 48

Child Care Aware of America, 14, 28–29, 31, 50, 58, 62, 81, 137, 119

Child Care for Working Families Act, 58–59

Child Care Resource and Referral networks, 124

Child safety and health, 109

Child-care deserts, 69–79

Child-care networks, 138–139

Child-care subsidy programs, 16–17, 31, 52–54, 61, 76–79, 96

Children in foster care, 48, 113–114, 119

Children with special needs, 10, 25
    barriers for child-care providers, 122–131
    barriers for families, 120–122
    case example, 127–131
    CCDBG requirements, 48
    coordinating services for, 97
    costs for providing care, 122
    developmental delays, 100, 113, 127
    Head Start, 114, 116
    in child care, 119–131
    inconsistent demand, 123
    public preschool, 95
    public school system, 91
    quality child care and, 57
    staff turnover and, 124
    state funding streams, 50
    subsidies for, 136–137
    supporting, 139
    suspension and expulsion, 124–127
    time for, 41
    training to provide care, 123–124
    underserved population, 73–74

Children's Bureau, 105–107

Class size, 17, 27–28

Company-assisted child care, 83

Co-op care, 59–60

Costs, 14, 50–51
    burden on families, 57–67
    decreasing income, increasing costs, 17–19
    different perspectives, 21–23
    for children with special needs, 120, 122
    infant and toddler vs. preschool, 18–19
    model for financial stability, 15–16

decreasing income, increasing cost, 17–19

lack of, 54–55, 69–79

model for financial stability, 15–16

rural vs. urban access, 70–72

searching for, 63–67

staff turnover, 19–21

vs. cost, 13–23

R

Regional cost differences, 58

Respect, 41, 134–135

    for child-care providers, 36–38

    for learning process, 38

    for partnership, 36–37

    for time, 37

    for value, 38

    lack of, 42–44

Rural vs. urban access to child care, 70–72

S

Social/emotional development, 1, 125–126

Social-media campaigns, 134

Speech disorders, 127

Staff turnover, 20–23, 30–31, 35–36, 117–118, 120, 124

State and national perspectives, 82–83

State funding streams, 49–50, 52, 54–55, 135–137

Supplemental Nutrition Assistance Program, 31, 85

Suspension and expulsion, 116, 124–127

T

Teacher training, 123–125, 135

Teachers

    attracting, 10

    child care vs. kindergarten, 4

    consequences of turnover, 30–31

    Head Start training, 115

    high expectations for, 25–28

    job responsibilities, 28–29

    lack of, 19–21

    living below poverty level, 31

    need for, 25–26

    professional development, 41

    raising salaries, 17

    responsibilities vs. wages, 3–4

    training, 17, 25, 47

    turnover, 19–21

Temporary Assistance for Needy Families, 49

Transportation, 93, 95–96, 98–100

Trauma, 119

Tuition affordability, 2–3

U

Uncollected income, 16, 38

Underserved populations, 72–75

    children who need care during nontraditional hours, 74–75

    children with special needs, 73–74

    infants and toddlers, 72–73

Unrealistic expectations, 43

V

Vision screening, 113

Voucher systems, 52–54

Vulnerable families, 115–118

W

Waiting lists, 63–64

War on Poverty, 113

Women, Infants, and Children program, 33–34

Working at home, 10

Z

Zoning laws, 137